# simply
# beautiful

# cards

## 50 QUICK AND
## EASY PROJECTS

### heidi boyd

**D&C**
David and Charles

A DAVID & CHARLES BOOK
David & Charles is a subsidiary of F+W (UK) Ltd.,
an F+W Publications Inc. company

First published in the UK in 2005
First published in the US by North Light Books, an
imprint of F+W Publications Inc, in 2005

A catalogue record for this book is available from the
British Library.

ISBN 0 7153 2055 6 paperback

Printed in China by Regent
for David & Charles
Brunel House    Newton Abbot    Devon

Visit our website at www.davidandcharles.co.uk

David & Charles books are available from all good
bookshops; alternatively you can contact our
Orderline on (0)1626 334555 or write to us at FREEP-
OST EX2 110, David & Charles Direct, Newton Abbot,
TQ12 4ZZ (no stamp required UK mainland).


Editor: David Oeters
Designer: Marissa Bowers
Layout Artists: Kathy Gardner and Donna Cozatchy
Production Coordinator: Robin Richie
Photographers: Christine Polomsky and Tim Grondin
Photo Stylist: Jan Nickum

## metric conversion chart

| TO CONVERT | TO | MULTIPLY BY |
| --- | --- | --- |
| Inches | Centimetres | 2.54 |
| Centimetres | Inches | 0.4 |
| Feet | Centimetres | 30.5 |
| Centimetres | Feet | 0.03 |
| Yards | Metres | 0.9 |
| Meters | Yards | 1.1 |
| Sq. Inches | Sq. Centimetres | 6.45 |
| Sq. Centimetres | Sq. Inches | 0.16 |
| Sq. Feet | Sq. Metres | 0.09 |
| Sq. Metres | Sq. Feet | 10.8 |
| Sq. Yards | Sq. Metres | 0.8 |
| Sq. Metres | Sq. Yards | 1.2 |
| Pounds | Kilograms | 0.45 |
| Kilograms | Pounds | 2.2 |
| Ounces | Grams | 28.4 |
| Grams | Ounces | 0.04 |

# ABOUT THE author

Artist **HEIDI BOYD** creates innovative craft projects for both children and adults, emphasizing the elements of surprise and accessibility. In addition to **SIMPLY BEAUTIFUL GREETING CARDS**, Heidi has authored **SIMPLY BEAUTIFUL BEADING**, **WIZARD CRAFTS**, **PET CRAFTS** and **FAIRY CRAFTS**, all published by North Light Books. She's contributed proprietary projects to **BETTER HOMES AND GARDENS** magazines and craft books.

With a degree in fine arts, Heidi has taught workshops and art classes in schools and art centers for over a decade. She lives in Maine with her husband, two sons and dog.

# DEDICATED TO...

My wonderful husband, Jon, whose fortieth birthday passed without a card while I was in the throes of designing projects for this book. Also to my boys, Jasper and Elliot, who understand why Mom spends countless hours in the studio. I'm so happy to have all three of you waiting for me when the work is over.

## acknowledgments • A big thank you to the talents and hard work of North Light's Christine Polomsky, David Oeters and Marissa Bowers. They took boxes of cards and pages of copy and transformed them into this Simply Beautiful book.

PEA

 # contents

INTRODUCTION 7

*getting started*
8

tools · 8

paper · 10

embellishments · 12

techniques · 14

    Making a blank card | 14

    Worrking with patterns | 15

    Worrking with stamps | 15

CHAPTER 1
## personal
16

    Fresh Produce | 18

    Beaded Flowers | 20

    Kite Card | 22

    Wild Kingdom Card | 24

    Cactus Card | 26

    Western Roundup | 28

    Blue Jeans Card | 30

    Sandy Paws | 32

    Sunflower Card | 34

    Beehive Card | 36

    Forever Yours | 38

    Two for Tea Card | 40

    Television Card | 42

    Fishbowl Card | 45

    Chinese Take-Out | 46

    Fortune Cookie Card | 49

    Victorian Bird Cage | 50

    Party Hats | 52

    What's Cooking? | 54

CHAPTER 2
## special event
56

    The Envelope, Please | 58

    Chic Paper Purse | 60

    Good Wishes | 62

    Little House Card | 64

    Wedding Cake Card | 66

    Wedding Dress Card | 68

    Make-a-Wish | 70

    Birthday Pin Card | 72

    Pretty Paper Cake | 74

    Little Feet | 76

    Baby Buggy Card | 78

    Baby Bib Card | 81

    Flower Power Card | 82

    Catch a Falling Star | 84

    Puzzle Card | 86

    Crazy Cat | 88

CHAPTER 3
## seasonal and holiday
90

    Hearts | 92

    Candy Heart | 94

    Snapshot | 96

    Carry-on | 99

    Tropical Escape | 100

    Gone Fishin' | 102

    Stamped Leaf Card | 104

    Spiderweb Card | 106

    Spinning Spider Card | 108

    Scaredy Cat Card | 111

    Snowflake Card | 112

    Rhinestone Tree | 114

    Cold Hands, Warm Hearts | 116

    Holiday Sparkle | 118

    Winter Wonderland | 122

RESOURCES 126

INDEX 127

FEELING GROOVY

# introduction

there's nothing like opening the mailbox and finding a handmade card amongst the junk mail and bills. The convenience of the Internet and cell phones has made stumbling upon such a treasure a rarity. In my experience, the time invested in making and sending handmade cards is greatly appreciated. It never ceases to amaze me how long handmade messages are cherished and remembered.

Tucked away in my drawer is a bundle of beautiful love letters that my husband sent me after we met. He hand lettered and colored the envelopes with such care that I knew they held special messages inside. I've carefully stashed away the cards our boys have drawn and written, hoping to hold on to moments of their childhood. Friends have sent handmade cards that I've displayed like artwork.

When I shared the idea for this book with my mum she dug out her own collection of cards. Inside was correspondence I sent when we lived in the Midwest. I was able to incorporate some of the ideas into this book. I've included favorites from teaching children's art classes and adult workshops. The wonderful papercrafting accessories that can be found in stores inspired many brand new card designs.

Over the years I've found that people are engaged and surprised by original cards, especially ones that are interactive or made with unexpected materials. You don't need to be an artist to assemble these clever cards. In these pages are patterns and step-by-step instructions that make card making simple. Pull out your scissors and glue and take the time to send a simply beautiful handmade card to someone you love.

# tools

It's easy to get carried away with the overwhelming selection of tools available in craft stores. To keep things simple I tried to stick with the basics, while still including some handy time savers. Before you begin cardmaking, assemble the basic supplies I've listed below, many of which you might already own. As you embark on new card designs you can slowly acquire the additional specialty tools in the individual material lists.

## basic tools

|EMBOSSING TOOL| Embossing tools are available with different sized metal balls on one or both of the ends. The larger sized ball end is ideal for scoring the center of the paper when folding a card. The smaller ball end is better for more detailed embossing or scoring fine lines. |MARKER| You'll need at least one reliable black marker. I find it helpful to have a fine-tip and a broad-tip marker when I craft. |PAPER TRIMMER| I used a 12" (30cm) craft paper trimmer. The ruled grid lines on a paper trimmer make cutting straight cards, rectangles, squares and paper strips a breeze. It's small enough to fit in the chaos of my work table, and the straightforward blade is easy to operate and replace. It's an indispensable tool for card making. |PENCIL| A sharp pencil can make card design easier. |RULER| Keep a simple straight-edged measuring tool close at hand, to cut trims to the appropriate length and to use as a guide for drawing or scoring along the straight edge. |SCISSORS| Having good scissors is essential to successful papercrafting. There's no greater frustration than dull scissors, or ones that are too big or small for the job. Sharp micro-tipped scissors are best for cutting in small areas. I'd also suggest a pair of soft touch spring scissors, which require very little cutting pressure.

## adhesives

Having the right adhesive for a project makes the job much easier. |PAPER GLUE| Aleene's 2 in 1 Glue is my glue of choice for lightweight papers. The broad tip evenly distributes a thin layer of glue over the paper. It's formulated to be repositionable, but dries permanent. It's acid free, xylene free and non-toxic. |SCRAPBOOK GLUE| I use Aleene's Memory Glue, which is ideal for gluing heavyweight paper, trims and embellishments. The narrow tip allows easy control of the glue flow, which is helpful when gluing small card embellishments. It's photo safe, acid free and nontoxic. |EMBELLISHMENT GLUE| Aleene's Platinum Bond Glass and Bead Slick Surfaces Adhesive is perfect for the jewelry-making techniques that were used in some of the cards. This strong glue is formulated to glue glass beads, metal and plastic together. |REPOSITIONABLE GLUE TAPE| Keep this adhesive handy for attaching transparent vellum, tissue paper and sheer ribbon lengths. Traditional glue might seep through these items or cause discoloration. Apply the tape sticky side down, then apply even pressure along the backing before peeling it off.

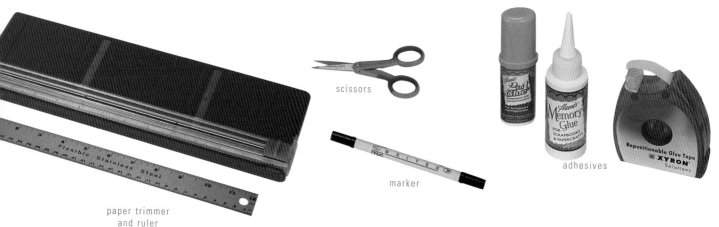

scissors

marker

adhesives

paper trimmer
and ruler

## paper punches

There is an endless variety of paper punches on the market. They are fun and easy to use, but can be costly. The ⅝" (2cm) and 1" (3cm) circle punches I consider to be essential. | **HAND PUNCHES** | Simply squeeze the handles of the hand punch together to make smaller sized circles and small stars. Hand punches are used throughout the book to assemble cards. You can find these punches in craft or office supply stores. | **STAND-ALONE PUNCHES** | Stand-alone punches rest on the table and pressure is applied to the top of the punch to cut out larger circles, hearts, stars and other shapes. These punches are found where papercrafting supplies are sold.

## other tools

| **AWL** | The small-sized awl has a narrow tip designed for papercrafting. In this book, the awl is used to pre-punch small holes through cardstock. | **BONE FOLDER** | A helpful tool to give handmade cards a more professional finish. Apply even pressure and swipe one of the smooth bone folder edges across scored paper to make a sharp fold line. | **CRAFT KNIFE** | Many projects call for the use of a craft knife. Make sure you have extra blades. A sharp blade requires less pressure and makes a safer cutting tool. | **DECORATIVE SCISSORS** | These scissors come in a whole host of patterns such as scallop and pinking edges. Quality is important when choosing scissors. Fiskars makes a streamlined decorative edge scissor that makes a clean cut. | **EYELET SETTER** | This is a metal rod with a rounded tip that's designed to penetrate the center of the eyelet. When tapped with a hammer, the setter guides the open edge of the eyelet to fold down against the paper. Be sure the size of the eyelet setter corresponds with the size of the eyelet. Use a small hammer, as a large hammer might damage the project. | **ROUNDNOSE PLIERS** | These are used primarily for shaping wire. The smooth, rounded ends easily grasp and manipulate the wire without marring the finish. | **SELF-HEALING CUTTING BOARD** | Keep a small cutting board close at hand to protect your work surface when using a craft knife, or to aid in scoring paper while using an embossing tool. The grid lines help line up both the paper and ruler while using either tool. | **SHAPE CUTTER AND SHAPE TEMPLATE** | Tools such as these make papercrafting simple. There are a variety of products on the market that perform this basic function, such as the Fiskars ShapeCutter. Move the cutter along the sides of the template to instantly cut out a shaped window. You'll never want to go back to using scissors or a craft knife to cut shapes again.

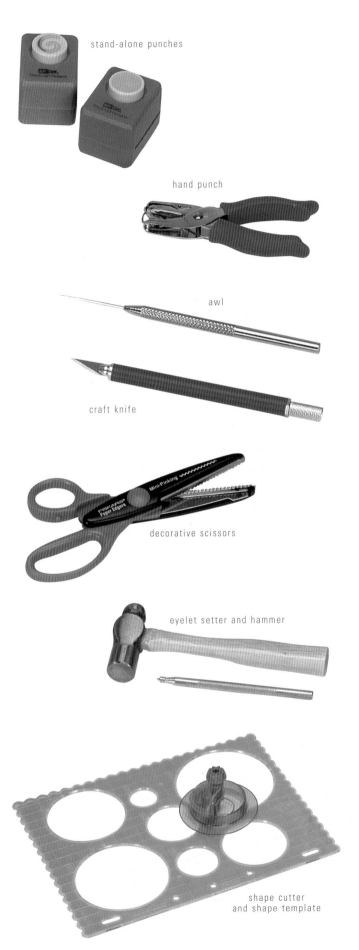

stand-alone punches

hand punch

awl

craft knife

decorative scissors

eyelet setter and hammer

shape cutter
and shape template

When shopping for supplies, I'm always stumbling upon appealing new textured and patterned papers. New paper products appear in stores all the time. What you'll find below is a sampling of the paper varieties on the market and some tips on how to get the most out of your paper when making cards.

## paper types

|ORIGAMI| Most often found in art supply and craft stores, these square sheets are intended for paper folding projects. Origami papers are perfect for card making. You can find origami paper that is metallic, mesh and patterned. There are origami papers that incorporate floral elements and fabric-like finishes. Affordably priced, the small-sized sheets are packaged in assorted colors. |TISSUE AND HANDMADE PAPER| Handmade tissue paper has long fibers and comes in a wide variety of translucent colors. It is soft and more flexible than traditional tissue paper. Rice paper is thinner, more opaque and has shorter fibers which allow it to tear easily. Handmade paper is solid, much thicker and has a very irregular surface that is soft and cottony to the touch. |CARDSTOCK| Heavier than copy paper, cardstock is used as a base for almost all the cards in the book. I would recommend stocking up on several mixed color packages of cardstock. Keep plenty of neutral colors on hand such as white, cream, tan and brown. Also look for two-color cardstock that features one color on the front and another color on the back. |VELLUM| Vellum is a very thin translucent paper. Handle it carefully! When creased it gets unsightly white lines. Besides solid color sheets, vellum comes printed with images, embossed with small patterns such as stars and spirals, and can incorporate glitter and sparkles for added flair. |PATTERNED SCRAPBOOK PAPER| Scrapbook paper sheets come in a variety of colors and patterns. They're inexpensive, so if you find one you like don't hesitate to pick it up and add it to your card making paper collection. If you're having trouble finding a specific paper that is used in the book, please keep in mind that paper patterns are often discontinued or replaced with new patterns. If you search for a suitable substitution, you'll most likely find something better! |TEXTURED PAPER| During the manufacturing process textured paper has been stamped with a relief that gives a solid color page a more interesting finish. From simple ribbing to elaborate diamond patterns, the textured paper selection is widely varied. |SUEDE PAPER| Fibers have been added to one side of this paper, making it very soft. Look for this paper in scrapbooking stores.

## finding & storing paper

Scrapbook stores specialize in selling individual letter size or 12" (30cm) square paper sheets. They are typically sorted by variety, subject and color. This is a convenient way to find specific colors and purchase a small quantity of specialty paper. Craft stores also sell individual scrapbook sheets, but they often carry mixed packages of colored and patterned copy and cardstock paper as well. Office supply stores sell economically priced reams of assorted solid colors of copy and cardstock papers. Art stores tend to carry large sheets of handmade, marbled and tissue papers. You may want to explore the cost savings of buying paper this way if you're planning to make multiple cards, espe-

origami papers

cially at Christmas time. If you're making individual cards, look for mixed bags of paper scraps in craft supply stores. You'll get a wide variety of small sized sheets for an economical price.

Another consideration when shopping for papers is acid content. Papers that are acid free will not deteriorate as quickly as those with acid content. To get the most out of your investment in acid-free paper, use only acid-free glues, markers and stickers to make a truly long lasting card.

Protect your investment by storing paper sheets flat. Although it's not archival safe, I prefer clear plastic storage containers. With a quick glance you can find what you're looking for. Clear plastic envelopes are perfect for storing a small quantity of paper, but for larger quantities, a stack of clear plastic boxes or drawers is ideal. I recommend sorting paper by variety to help keep your paper collection in order. A little bit of paper can go a long way when making cards. Just one sheet of patterned paper can be used in six or seven cards. Save time and money by carefully storing your scraps.

## other paper products

|HOLOGRAPHIC STICKER SHEETS| These stickers are sold by individual sheet and are extremely easy to use. Use them in conjunction with patterns to create your own stickers. These sheets can be found at scrapbooking and craft supply stores. |PICTURE STICKERS AND DIMENSIONAL STICKERS| Take advantage of the many beautiful stickers that are available and use them as a focal point of the card or as an accent for decoration. Stickers come in a variety of finishes, such as flat, clear, metallic and translucent. Clear dimensional stickers spotlight an image or message. |PRE-FOLDED CARDS| A great short cut I've discovered is blank cards that are sold packaged with envelopes or in "stackers." Stackers are a notepad of pre-scored cards, just tear one off and fold. Manufactured cards are not a necessity, since you can easily make your own with cardstock. However, they're worth the expense as they save time and let you enjoy the fun of decorating right away. You can find blank cards in craft and scrapbook stores, especially where rubber stamps are sold. |ENVELOPES| This book focuses on cards, and there wasn't room left for handmade envelopes. However, some of the card designs do have suggestions for decorating manufactured envelopes to match the cards. Colored card-sized envelopes can be bought in singles, pairs or small packs at craft stores and scrapbook stores. If you need larger quantities or business-sized envelopes check out the selection in stationery stores.

A VARIETY OF PAPER

# embellishments

The growing popularity of scrapbooking has brought a wonderful array of specialty papercrafting notions to the market. Mini brads, rivets and thin wires are great assets to card making. Whenever you add embellishments to a card you'll add weight, so be sure to place additional postage on the envelope.

## *embellishments*

| MINI BRAD FASTENERS | They work just like their standard sized counterparts but they're less cumbersome, making them perfect for card making. They're widely available in both silver and gold colors. | EYELETS | Eyelets come in a whole host of sizes, colors and finishes. They're sold with specialty papercrafting supplies. Make sure you have an eyelet setter that fits the size eyelet you purchase. | BUTTONS | Select flat or low profile buttons to use on your cards. Some companies are manufacturing buttons exclusively for papercrafts. They are often made of plastic and don't have holes, since they will be glued in place. | BEADS | Small glass seed beads are well suited for decorating paper cards. Larger bead varieties are often too bulky to mail, and may puncture the envelope. | WIRE | The higher the gauge is, the thinner the wire. Take advantage of the variety of colored wire available in both the jewelry and paper-crafting sections of craft stores. | MESH | Wireform wire

mesh is manufactured in a variety of sizes, metal colors, weaves and patterns. You can also find thin metal sheets that work like mesh. I use the finest or lightest gauge wire mesh for cards. Small gauge mesh has the added benefit of being easily cut with regular scissors. | RIBBON | Like icing on the cake, ribbon often adds the finishing touch of color to a card. I've primarily used thin ribbons ⅛" (3mm) to ¼" (6mm) wide in an attempt to help reduce the bulk of the finished card. | SILK FLOWERS | Silk ribbon roses can be purchased stitched to a straight ribbon, or loose in cellophane packages. Locate them in the sewing notions department in fabric stores or with ribbons in the floral department of craft stores. They're available in different colors and sizes. Select the variety that works with your paper colors. | EMBROIDERY FLOSS | Inexpensive and readily available in a multitude of colors, embroidery floss often comes in handy when making mixed-media cards.

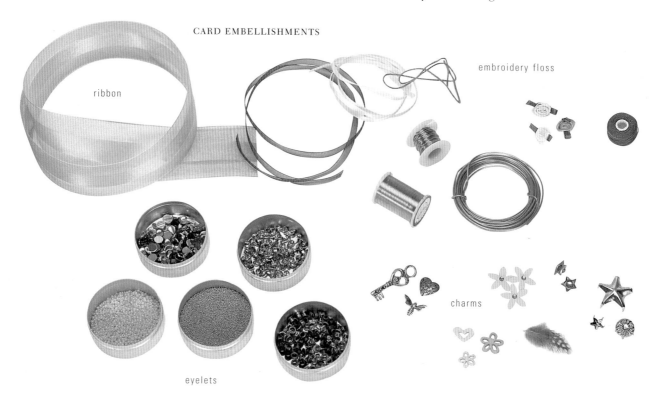

CARD EMBELLISHMENTS

ribbon

embroidery floss

charms

eyelets

# type

There are many different ways to incorporate type into your card-making project. Each of these methods has its advantages and disadvantages. Experiment to find which one works best for you.

| **HANDWRITING** | Nothing could be easier and more personal than picking up a pen and handwriting your sentiments. If you're comfortable, simply write your greeting directly on the card. If you're unsure, test your handwriting on scrap paper and then place it over the card to check the effect before writing on the finished card.

| **COMPUTER-GENERATED TYPE** | The computer allows you to write custom messages in many typefaces. Both the size and color of the type can be changed with a simple click of a button. Experiment with printing on different colored paper. When you're pleased with the results, trim the message and glue it to the card. Sometimes the perfection of computer-generated type is an attractive contrast to the inherent irregularities in a handmade card. | **ALPHABET OR LETTER STAMPS** | Unlike computer-generated type, individual stamp letters have a handcrafted appearance, but are more uniform than hand lettering. You may compose your own messages with the stamps, making them perfect for every holiday or special occasion. Invest in both a lowercase and uppercase alphabet stamp set so you have at least two sizes to combine and choose from. Because hand stamping is sometimes inconsistent, always test print on scrap paper. There's nothing worse than ruining a finished card by making an unforeseen stamping error. Try to stamp the message first and then decorate the card. | **MESSAGE STAMPS** | These are the easiest text stamps to use as each word is perfectly spaced and printed in a single motion. Select generic messages, like *thank you* and *best wishes*, that can be used for many cards. | **STICKERS** | Like stamps, individual letter stickers allow you the freedom to create your own messages. Whole word message stickers are easier to apply. Instead of lining up each individual letter, they're applied in a single motion.

*tip* > You can add sentiments to any card in this book. You'll find a list of message suggestions with many of the projects.

TYPE EMBELLISHMENTS

stamps

stickers

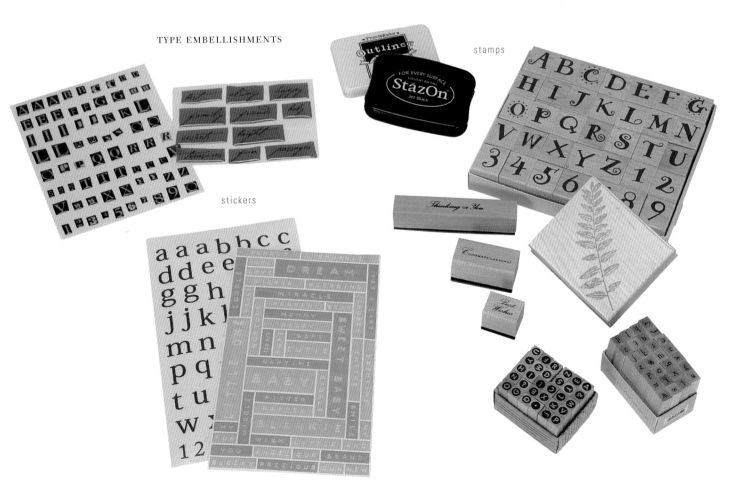

# techniques

Papercrafting is easy if you can trace, cut, fold and glue. With a few simple skills, you're well on your way to successfully making the cards in this book. These techniques will help take the guesswork out of getting started.

## *Making a blank card*

If the card you're working on isn't standard size, or you're not using a manufactured blank card, follow these steps to make your own professional-looking blank cards.

One • Use a paper trimmer to cut the paper to the required size. While trimming, make sure the paper edges are aligned with the ruled grid lines to ensure the cut paper is square.

two • Position the paper over a cutting board and align the paper edges with the grid lines. Use a pencil to mark the exact center of the paper on the top and bottom edges. Lay the ruler across the paper and align its top edge with the pencil marks and the grid lines. Draw the embossing tool across the ruler while applying steady pressure to the paper to make an even score line.

three • Fold the paper in half along the score line, making sure the side and bottom edges match up. Swipe the side edge of the bone folder across the fold.

*tip* > Take credit for your cards by stamping or signing your initials on the back cover. The recipient will know you made the card despite its professional appearance.

# Working with patterns

Patterns make it easy to assemble beautiful cards simply and quickly. I've included a few simple steps to help you get the most out of the patterns in this book.

 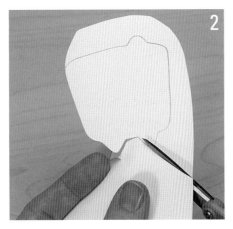 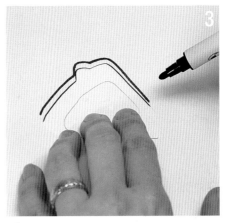

one · Trace or copy the pattern included with the project on cardstock. Use the cardstock shape to trace the pattern on the paper surface you will use in the project. Make sure to draw the pattern on the side of the paper that will not be seen.

two · To use the pattern for your card, cut out the pattern from the paper. Trim away the excess paper. In tight areas, cut from the outside in, instead of turning the scissors and damaging the pattern.

three · To add dimension to the cut patterns you might have to edge the pattern in black marker. To do this lay the pattern over scrap paper and run the edge of the black felt-tip marker along the outside edge of the pattern. This also serves to hide uneven edges and tracing blemishes.

# Working with stamps

Rubber stamping is one of the easiest ways to add an image or type to your work. Here's a few quick tips to get you started stamping.

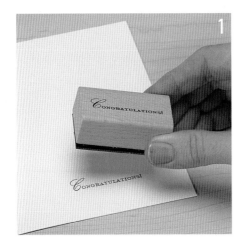

one · Tap the stamp on the ink pad. Make sure ink covers the entire image. Press the stamp firmly on the surface, making sure not to wiggle so that the entire image is pressed evenly. Lift the stamp carefully in one smooth motion.

tip > Follow the instructions to enlarge or reduce the pattern if necessary. Make note of any fold, score or punch lines that are marked on the pattern; the instructions may have you refer to them to accurately assemble the card. Save the cardstock patterns to use for future cards. If you are making many cards, you may want to use a heavier cardstock.

# personal

**a**s the saying goes, "one picture is worth a thousand words." These clever cards are the perfect way to express your feelings. Whether you're sending an informative letter to a friend or making a declaration of true love to a soul mate, you can find the card design that suits your style, expresses your feelings or relates a special shared memory.

The personal cards in this chapter offer a wide range of choices. The *What's Cooking*, *Sunflower* and *Tea For Two* cards would be perfect for the homebodies in your life. Whereas the adventurous, out-door-types may prefer a *Sandy Paws* or *Wild Kingdom* card. The *Victorian Bird Cage* and *Forever Yours* cards set the stage for serious romantic expressions. You'll also find cards better suited for more casual expressions of love, such as the *Fortune Cookie* card and *Television* card.

Once you've selected a card design, don't hesitate to alter the paper patterns, charms or images. You'll find all handmade cards are easy to customize. Taking these extra steps to make a truly thoughtful card will show just how much you care.

**CHAPTER**

**1**

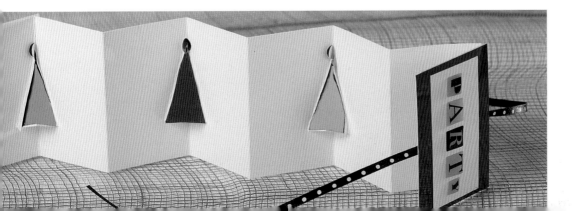

# fresh produce

## MATERIALS

8½" x 5½" (22cm x 14cm) cream colored cardstock, folded to a 4¼" x 5½" (11cm x 14cm) card

pea pod pattern cut from green textured paper

background pattern cut from ribbed white paper

1¾" x 2¾" (4cm x 7cm) black paper

1½" x 2¼" (4cm x 6cm) gold wire mesh

mini green buttons

1½" (4cm) green wire

alphabet letter stamps and black stamp pad

scrapbook glue

basic tools (see page 8)

### MESSAGES

*Berry, Pea, Peas In a Pod, Sweet Pea*

ANOTHER SIMPLY BEAUTIFUL IDEA

Ripe for the picking! This mixed-media card is a tempting work of art. Paper scraps combined with bits of buttons and wire come together to make luscious looking veggies.

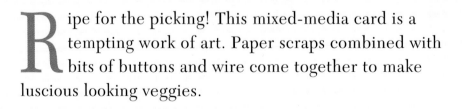

**Cut a strawberry out of polka dotted red scrapbook paper. Make seed holes in the strawberry with a ¹⁄₁₆" (2mm) circle hole punch. Glue a gold metallic paper behind the strawberry. Cut a small green leaf top and glue it on top of the strawberry. Use scrapbook glue to mount the finished strawberry over the prepared mesh and black paper background. Refer to the pattern on page 19.**

one • Using the black paper piece as a base, glue a piece of cut wire mesh on top of the black paper, and then glue the ribbed white paper on top of the mesh. Glue the pea pod pattern onto the white paper, then glue four green buttons onto the pea. Finally, make three loops in the wire to shape it into a stem and glue one end to the top of the pea.

two • Glue the finished pea pod to the front of the note card and then use letter stamps to label the vegetable.

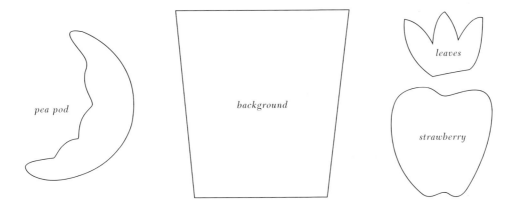

*pea pod*

*background*

*leaves*

*strawberry*

*Background cut from white ribbed paper and the pea pod from green textured paper. For the variation, the strawberry cut from red polka-dotted scrapbook paper, and the leaves from green scrapbook paper. Patterns are full size.*

# beaded flowers

## MATERIALS

4¾" x 9½" (12cm x 24cm) cream colored cardstock, folded to a 4¾" x 4¾" (12cm x 12cm) card

½" (1cm) wide purple paper strip

1½" (4cm) wide and 4½" (11cm) long purple and green ribbon

16" (41cm) length of 32-gauge silver beading wire for each flower

three purple *e* beads

green, purple and pearl colored seed beads

embellishment adhesive

double-stick tape

paper glue

basic tools (see page 8)

These shimmering flowers are beautiful beaded jewelry for your cards. Multiple loops of beads quickly bloom into round flower heads. Simply switch bead colors to make a variety of flowers. Unlike most manufactured beaded baubles for papercrafts, these are both inexpensive and low profile for easy mailing.

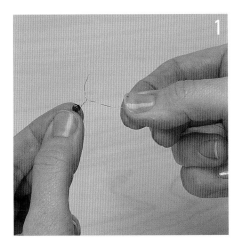

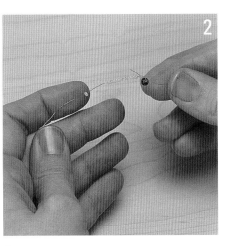

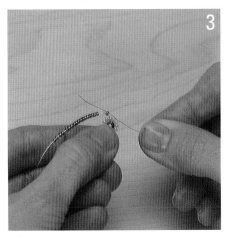

**one** · String an *e* bead flower center onto one end of the wire, then twist the wire end around itself to secure.

**two** · String twelve pearl seed beads onto the wire, then thread the wire end back through the first seed bead. Pull up the wire end to tighten the first petal ring around the flower center.

**three** · String twenty-four purple seed beads onto the wire, and then thread the wire back through the first purple bead to make the second petal ring.

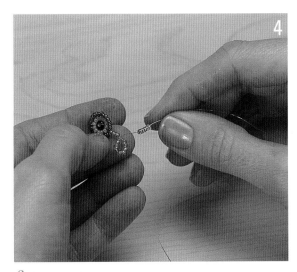

**four** · String sixteen green seed beads onto the wire end to make the stem. Twist eight of the stem beads into a loop to make a leaf. Secure the flower stem by wrapping the wire around itself just above the last green bead. Trim the excess wire. Repeat this process to create two more flowers, using different colors.

**five** · Orient the card so that the fold is at the top. Trim ¼" (1cm) off the bottom edge of the card cover. Working inside the card, glue the purple paper strip to the bottom edge so that it's visible when the card is closed. Apply double-stick tape to the underside of the ribbon and mount it across the front of the card, aligning the bottom edge of the ribbon with the bottom edge of the trimmed card cover. Arrange the flowers over the right side of the ribbon and then apply embellishment adhesive to the underside of the flower heads to anchor them in place. Allow the glue to set before mailing.

# kite card

## MATERIALS

8" x 9½" (20cm x 24cm) light blue striped scrapbook paper, folded to a 4" x 9½" (10cm x 24cm) card

4" x 9½" (10cm x 24cm) cloud patterned vellum

4" x 9½" (10cm x 24cm) cloud patterned paper

business-sized envelope

kite pattern cut from white textured paper

triangle pattern cut from blue paper

tail pattern pieces cut from green, red and yellow textured paper

white thread

blue adhesive scrapbook letters

standard hole punch

sewing machine

double-stick tape

paper glue

basic tools (see page 8)

## MESSAGES

*Soar, Fly, Hello*

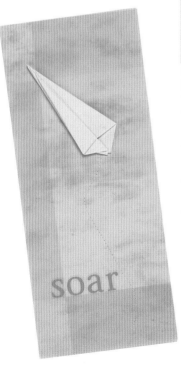

Lift spirits with this high-flying card. Sew paper layers together with a line of stitching that becomes the kite tail and strings. Machine sewing through paper is easier than you think; the machine clamps layers together and swiftly glides them under the needle. Give this technique a try. You'll love the professional-looking results.

## ANOTHER SIMPLY BEAUTIFUL IDEA

You won't need any pattern pieces for this card, just fold a miniature paper airplane from a 4" x 2" (10cm x 5cm) white paper scrap. Make a single wavy line of stitching towards the center of the card, beginning two thirds of the way up from the base. Glue the underside of the airplane to the top end of the stitching.

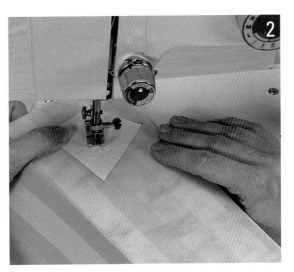

one · Use paper glue to attach the cloud paper sheet inside the card. Apply a small strip of double-sided adhesive to both the top and bottom of the vellum sheet and affix it to the front of the card.

two · Thread the sewing machine with white thread and test stitch through scrap paper. Open the card and position the white kite pattern in the right hand corner of the front of the card. Stitch from the top of the kite (through both the vellum and paper card covers) down the center of the kite. End the line of stitching with a 2" (5cm) long curved tail below the kite. For the kite string make a second line of stitching that starts at the center of the kite and ends at the right edge of the card. Trim the threads and glue them inside the card to prevent the stitching from unraveling.

three · Glue two blue triangles to opposite corners of the white kite. Glue the tail pieces ½" (1cm) to ¾" (2cm) apart along the stitched tail. Punch a circle out of the red, yellow and green paper scraps and glue one to each of the tail pieces. Apply letter stickers to the bottom of the card to spell a message. As an option, create a matching envelope. First glue a 3½" x 2½" (9cm x 6cm) piece of scrapbook paper to the bottom right hand corner of the envelope, then apply letter stickers across the envelope and decorative paper.

*kite*

*triangles*

*tail pieces*

*Enlarge 135%. Kite cut from white textured paper, and tail pieces cut from green, red and yellow textured paper.*

# wild kingdom card

## MATERIALS

### ZEBRA CARD

5½" x 8" (14cm x 20cm) white
cardstock, folded to a 5½" x 4"
(14cm x 10cm) card

3⅛" x 2½" (8cm x 6cm)
black textured paper

3" x 2⅜" (8cm x 6cm)
green textured paper

5½" x 2¾" (14cm x 7cm) gold and green
patterned paper

2½" x 1⅞" (6cm x 5cm) lightweight
metal sheet (ArtEmboss)

wild animal sticker

embossing tool

double-stick tape

paper glue

basic tools (see page 8)

### ENVELOPE

white envelope

¾" x 3½" (2cm x 9cm)
black textured paper

3½"x 2¼" (9cm x 6cm)
green textured paper

3¼" x 2⅛"" (8cm x 5cm) white paper

wild animal sticker

### MESSAGES

*Run Wild, Stand Tall, Be Strong*

Stand
Tall

**T**his exotic card starts with a single sticker that's trans-
formed into a work of art when it's mounted onto a
metal sheet and framed with decorative papers. Use
the image as inspiration for the message inside.

ANOTHER SIMPLY
BEAUTIFUL
IDEA

Change the orientation of the card and the message to
match the animal sticker you choose. For this card I
used a giraffe and added green textured paper for
grass below the sticker.

one · Apply a zebra sticker to the center of the metal square, then use the embossing tool and ruler to make an impressed line around the inside edge of the metal.

two · Glue the green paper over the black paper, lining up the bottom and right edges of the green and black papers. Apply double stick tape to the underside of the metal square and then mount it diagonally across the green paper.

three · Orient the card horizontally and use glue to mount the gold and green paper across the front of the card. Apply more glue to the underside of the black paper and then position it in the lower center portion of the gold and green paper strip.

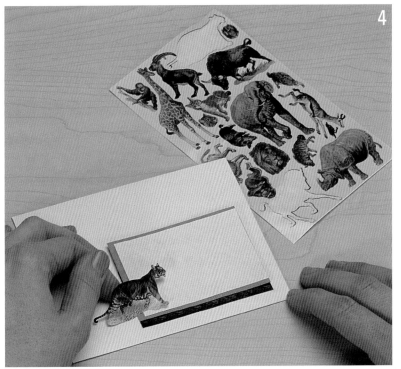

four · Use glue to attach the following paper pieces to the envelope; the black strip to the lower right corner of the envelope, the green rectangle above the black strip and the white rectangle centered over the green rectangle. Apply an animal sticker to the left edge of the finished address label.

# cactus card

Y ou can almost feel the heat wave of saturated color emanating from this southwestern note card. Glowing sun and waves of sand are the perfect setting for the towering cactus. Punched holes, drawn spikes and a blooming silk flower bring the cut paper cactus to life.

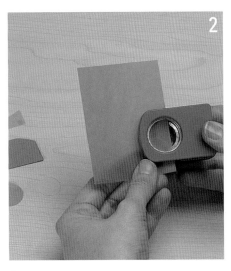

one · Punch three rows of holes down the central stem of the cactus, then punch two rows of holes down each of the offshoot branches. Connect the holes with a broken line of metallic gold marker. Then use a fine-tip black marker to randomly draw short spikes coming out from some of the holes.

two · Cut out the sand from brown and tan cardstock. Use the ½" (1cm) circle punch and yellow cardstock to make the sun. Use the 1" (3cm) circle punch and orange vellum to make the sun's background and then with the same punch make a partial circle opening in the right edge of the blue vellum sky.

three · Use paper glue to attach the following pieces to the front of the turquoise card; mount the blue vellum sky to the center, position the brown sand background over the bottom edge of the sky, and then insert the orange vellum sun background into the punched opening in the sky.

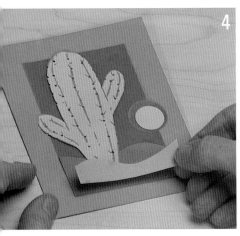

five · Cut two small silk flowers off the stem and then pull out the plastic flower centers so you're left with two silk petal rings. Use scrapbook glue to attach both petal rings and a rhinestone flower center to the cactus.

four · Use paper glue to attach the remaining paper pattern pieces; mount the cactus over the left side of the sky and sand background so the tip extends above the top edge of the sky. Add the yellow sun to the bottom of the orange sun background. Add the tan sand foreground, lining the bottom edge of the brown sand background and trapping the cactus base between the two sand layers.

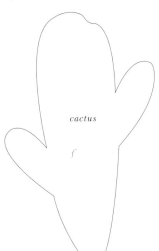

*cactus*

*sand foreground*

*sand background*

*Enlarge to 154%. Cactus cut from green cardstock, and the sand from brown and tan cardstock.*

# western roundup

## MATERIALS

5½" x 8½" (14cm x 22cm) cream colored cardstock, folded to a 5½" x 4¼" (14cm x 11cm) card

¾" (2cm) wide and 5½" (14cm) long strip of western printed scrapbook paper

cowboy hat pattern cut from simulated leather scrapbook paper

hat band pattern cut from tan suede paper

remaining hat pattern pieces cut from dark brown suede paper

⅛" (3mm) bronze star eyelet

small yellow and brown feather

eyelet setter and small hammer

paper glue

scrapbook glue

basic tools (see page 8)

## MESSAGES

*Giddyap, Yeee-Haaa!,
Howdy Partner*

Throw your hat into the ring... or mail! Send a howdy on this cowboy inspired card. It's the perfect greeting to send your country loving friends.

**one** · Orient the card horizontally, and trim ⅝" (2cm) from the bottom edge of the card cover. Working inside the card, use paper glue to attach the western paper strip along the bottom edge.

**two** · Apply paper glue to the underside of the simulated leather paper hat pattern and mount it to the center of the card cover. Use scrapbook glue to add the four brown suede pieces to the hat.

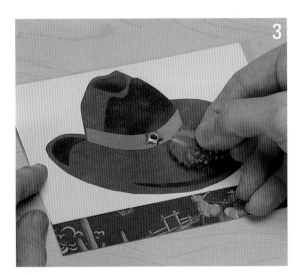

**three** · Use scrapbook glue to attach the tan hat band. Carefully puncture the hat brim and the front of the card with an awl, then thread the star eyelet into the hole. Working inside the card, use the eyelet setter and small hammer to flatten the eyelet against the inside card cover. Close the card and slip the feather quill into the wet glue under the hat brim.

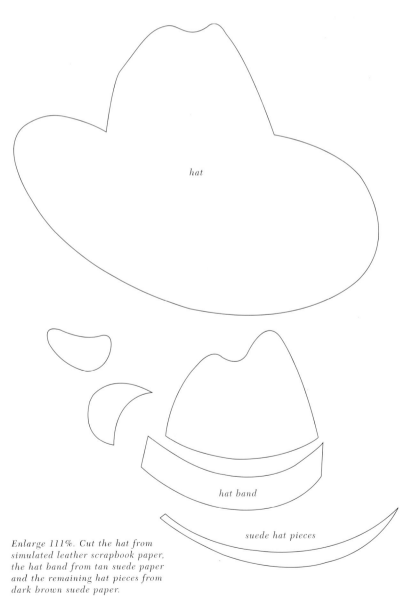

*hat*

*hat band*

*suede hat pieces*

*Enlarge 111%. Cut the hat from simulated leather scrapbook paper, the hat band from tan suede paper and the remaining hat pieces from dark brown suede paper.*

# blue jeans card

8" x 5½" (20cm x 14cm) white cardstock, folded to a 4" x 5½" (10cm x 14cm) card

jean patterns cut from denim printed scrapbook paper (or blue paper)

2¾" x 4" (7cm x 10cm) rectangle of striped scrapbook paper

pink embroidery floss

button

heart button

darning needle

craft knife

paper glue

scrapbook glue

basic tools (see page 8)

## MESSAGES

*Have a Hip and Happy Day, Feeling Groovy, True Blue Friend*

FEELING GROOVY

ANOTHER SIMPLY BEAUTIFUL IDEA

C asual and fun, these hip little cards are paper doll fashions for grown-ups. Retro bell-bottoms are cut from denim printed paper, then dressed up with embroidery floss and buttons. Add a groovy colored piece of scrapbook paper to the envelope to finish it off. They make this whimsical card perfect for lighthearted greetings.

**Make an individual fashion statement by cutting the pattern out of different paper. Experiment with applying fringe to the pant hems and switching embellishments.**

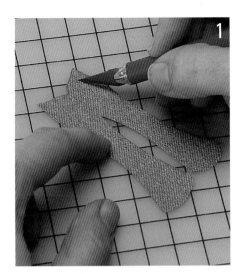

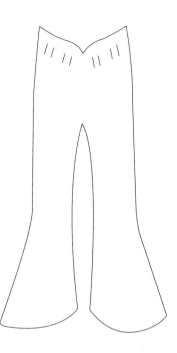

one · Use a craft knife to cut four belt loops along the waist of the blue jeans. Each loop is made with two small slits, see the pattern for exact placement.

two · Thread the needle with the embroidery floss and start stitching the belt from the center front of the jeans. Pass the needle through the two belt loops on the left side of the jeans. Bring the floss behind the jeans and then thread the needle through the two remaining belt loops on the right side. Remove the needle and tie the floss ends together in an overhand knot. If necessary, trim the ends of the floss.

*Blue jeans cut from denim scrapbook paper. Pattern is full size.*

three · Use paper glue to mount the rectangle of striped paper to the center of the note card, then glue the jeans over the center of the striped paper.

four · Use scrapbook glue to add a miniature button above the knotted belt and a heart button to the knee. Allow the glue to set completely before mailing.

# sandy paws

## MATERIALS

8½" x 5½" (22cm x 14cm) brown card-stock, folded to a 4¼" x 5½" (11cm x 14cm) card

neutral-toned cardstock

coral thread

colored pencils

sewing machine

basic tools (see page 8)

P ure happiness! Dogs love the freedom of running on long stretches of sandy beaches. Use this technique to share the joy of the moment in your favorite snap shots. Experiment with printing photographs on neutral-colored papers and artfully accenting the image with colored pencils.

one · Make a color copy of a photograph on neutral-toned cardstock. With colored pencils add small touches of color to the subject and broad sweeping strokes of color to the background.

two · Decide where you'll crop the image and draw pencil lines to mark the area.

three · Slowly tear along the crop lines to intentionally leave an uneven edge.

four · Thread the sewing machine with coral thread and test stitch through scrap paper. Stitch the torn photo to the front of the brown cardstock, starting and ending at the top right hand corner. When finished, cut the thread and let a couple of inches hang over the front of the card.

# sunflower card

## MATERIALS

11" x 5½" (28cm x 14cm) natural colored cardstock, folded to a 5½" x 5½" (14cm x 14cm) card

4⅞" x 5⅛" (12cm x 13cm) yellow striped paper

yellow cardstock

sunflower pattern cut from orange cardstock

tiny gold mini marbles

metal bee embellishments

off-white scrapbook alphabet stickers

scallop-edged scissors

paper glue

scrapbook glue

double-sided adhesive sheets

basic tools (see page 8)

### MESSAGES

*Sun, Flower, Summer, Wishing You Sun-Filled Days!*

Spread the warmth of summertime with this sunny greeting card. Shades of yellow paper are accented with miniature glittering gold marbles and metal bees. To keep things simple and bright I added a single word message with oversized off-white scrapbook letters.

one • Use scallop edged scissors to cut a 2⅛" (5cm) circle out of yellow cardstock. Cut a 2" (5cm) circle of double-sided adhesive. Peel off one side of the paper backing and apply the adhesive to the center of the scallop edged circle. Press flat, then remove the remaining paper backing.

two • Working over a dish, pour tiny gold mini marbles on to the exposed adhesive. When done, tap the finished flower center over the dish to collect any stray marbles.

three • Use scrapbook glue to attach the flower center to the middle of the cut orange sunflower. Use paper glue to mount the striped paper to the front of the card, and then glue the finished sunflower to the center of the striped paper.

four • Use scrapbook glue to attach two metal bee embellishments to the gold marble flower center. Spell the word *sun* with alphabet letter stickers across the bottom right edge of the petals and striped paper. Let the glue set completely before mailing.

*Enlarge 143%. Sunflower cut from orange cardstock.*

# beehive card

11" x 5½" (28cm x 14cm) natural colored cardstock, folded to a 5½" x 5½" (14cm x 14cm) card

beehive stripes cut from brown paper

beehive patter cut from textured beige paper

tiny gold mini marbles

metal bee embellishment

paper flowers with rhinestone centers

off-white scrapbook alphabet stickers

double-sided adhesive sheets

scrapbook glue

basic tools (see page 8)

## MESSAGES

*Bzz, Honey, Busy as a Bee, Sweet*

Is anyone you know busy as a bee? Send this card to their hive of activity. This card uses tiny gold mini marbles and bees to give the card an interesting texture. The addition of miniature rhinestone flowers adds a touch of sunshine to the hive.

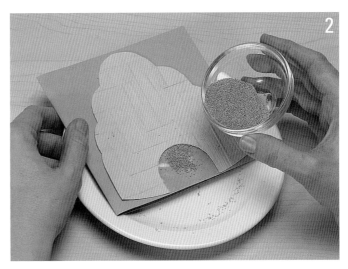

one · Working on the underside of the cut paper hive, stick a wide strip of double-sided adhesive across the arched opening. Apply glue to the top half of the hive and then turn the hive right side up and press it on the center of the card.

two · Working over a dish, pour tiny glass marbles over the exposed adhesive in the opening of the beehive. When done, tap the beehive over the dish to collect any stray marbles.

three · Glue three strips of cut brown paper between the ridges in the beehive. Decorate the card by gluing paper flowers and metal bee embellishments to the top and bottom of the hive. Create a message with alphabet letter stickers across the center of the hive.

*Enlarge 125%. Beehive pattern cut from textured beige paper.*

# forever yours

## MATERIALS

4¾" (12cm) square specialty card with attached metal tag (Paper Reflections) see tip for substitutions

tan scrapbook paper

metal heart-shaped lock and key embellishments

computer and printer

paper trimmer

scrapbook glue

paper glue

basic tools (see page 8)

### MESSAGES

*Forever Yours, Happy Anniversary, only you, Congratulations!*

ANOTHER SIMPLY BEAUTIFUL IDEA

Chronicle your sentiments of love inside these unique cards. Reminiscent of old library card catalogues, the framed messages are designed to look like they were made on an old typewriter. The embellishments are timeless symbols of devotion— heart, lock and key.

**This card style is perfect for special occasions! Just change the message and choose embellishments that reflect the sentiment.**

**one** · Use a computer to print a message using 18pt New Courier type onto the tan scrapbook paper, and then use a paper trimmer to cut the message slightly smaller than the label frame.

*tip* > For this project, I used blank cards that came with silver tags already attached. You can cut your own label frame out of silver paper and mount it to the front of the card with mini brads. Another option is to purchase printed paper hardware or adhesive sticker frames. Both are widely available where specialty scrapbooking supplies are sold.

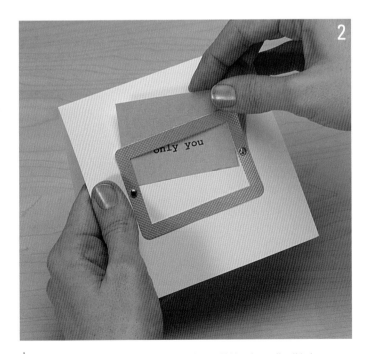

**two** · Slip the message into the label frame. If it's a loose fit, slide it out, apply paper glue to the underside of the tan cardstock, and then reinsert.

**three** · Use scrapbook glue to add a key and heart lock embellishments above the printed message. Allow the glue to set completely before mailing.

# two for tea card

## MATERIALS

12" x 5¼" (30cm x 13cm) green cardstock

2½" x 5¼" (6cm x 13cm) tan paper table

tea cup and saucer patterns cut from two varieties of pink and cream patterned scrapbook papers

5" (13cm) diameter white paper doily

tea bag

twine

message stamp and black stamp pad

embossing tool

¹⁄₁₆" (2mm) paper punch

paper glue

basic tools (see page 8)

### MESSAGES

*Thinking of You, Happy Mother's Day, Thank You Very Much!*

Tucked into the inner pocket of this card is an individually wrapped tea bag. The perfect card for someone who'd appreciate a quiet moment with a steaming cup of freshly brewed tea. For an added treat, include an invitation to a tea room. Few can resist cake with their tea.

**one** • Use a ruler and embossing tool to score the green cardstock at 5" (13cm) to make the top fold, and then again at 10" (25cm) to make the pocket fold. Fold the card cover down and stamp the message in black ink below the top fold.

**two** • Open the card and fold up the 2" (5cm) pocket. Punch three holes on both sides of the pocket. Space them a ½" (1cm) apart and position them ⅛" (3mm) from the outside edge. Stitch the sides of the pocket closed by stringing a piece of twine through each set of holes. Knot and trim the ends of the twine.

**three** • Close the card and glue the tan paper table to the front of the card, aligning it with the bottom and side edges of the card. Cut the doily in half, and glue the half-doily tablecloth over the center of the table.

**four** • Create the cups and saucers from a combination of the two patterned papers and glue them on the tablecloth.

**five** • Open the card and slide the other half of the doily, cut side down, into the pocket. Slip a tea bag over the doily.

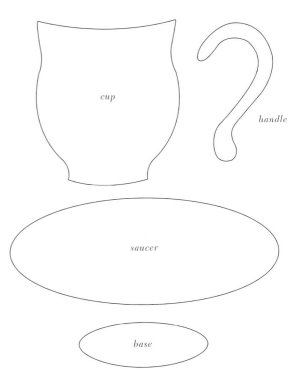

*cup*

*handle*

*saucer*

*base*

*Cup and saucer pattern pieces cut from pink and cream scrapbook pattern papers. Pattern is full size.*

# television card

## MATERIALS

3½" x 10" (9cm x 25cm) blue cardstock, folded to a 3½" x 5" (9cm x 13cm) card

TV pattern cut from white cardstock

inside TV screen pattern cut from simulated tie-dye printed scrapbook paper

clear plastic window (recycle heavyweight cellophane used in packaging)

dimensional clear plastic oval sticker

metallic heart sticker

2½" (6cm) length of 24-gauge white wire

black felt-tip marker

tape

scrapbook glue

paper glue

basic tools (see page 8)

Tune in for the special effects in this card that give a flat card real dimension. It's easier than it looks! A cut paper opening in the card is backed with clear cellophane and topped with a dimensional sticker. The window distorts the colored scrapbook paper mounted inside the card.

one · Cut the television pattern on page 44 out with scissors, and then use a craft knife to cut out the screen. Use black marker to outline the outer edge of the television including the domed antenna base. Lay the prepared television over the front of the blue card and use a pencil to trace around the inside edge of the screen opening.

two · Set the television aside, and with a craft knife cut the screen opening out of the blue card. To ensure the opening is large enough, be sure to cut along the outside edge of the pencil line.

three · Flip the card over and tape a small cellophane screen over the underside of the cut opening.

four · Cut a piece of tie-dye printed scrapbook paper slightly larger than the screen opening. Use paper glue to attach the cut paper inside the card. Close the card to check that it fills the cellophane screen. If necessary, readjust its placement before the glue sets.

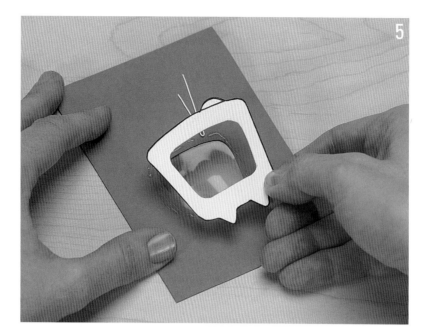

**five** · Fold the wire slightly off center to make an uneven television antenna. Working on the card cover, apply a dot of scrapbook glue just above the top right hand corner of the screen, place the folded wire end into the glue. Apply paper glue to the underside of the cut out television. Mount the television directly over the cut opening so that the edges line up to reveal the cellophane screen and tie-dye paper underneath.

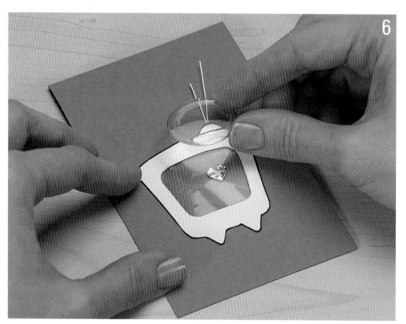

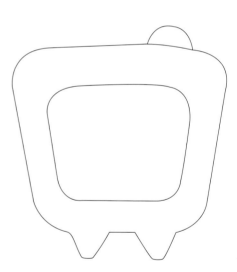

*TV cut from white cardstock.*
*Pattern is full size.*

**six** · Apply a heart sticker to the right side of the cellophane screen and then apply the dimensional oval sticker over the heart sticker, centering it on the cellophane screen.

# fishbowl card

## MATERIALS

3½" x 10" (9cm x 25cm)
orange cardstock, folded to a 3½" x 5"
(9cm x 13cm) card

fishbowl pattern cut from white
cardstock

simulated blue water printed scrapbook
paper

blue cardstock scraps

clear plastic window

metallic fish stickers

dimensional clear plastic oval sticker

black felt-tip marker

⅛" (3mm) hole punch

clear tape

paper glue

basic tools (see page 8)

*Enlarge 118%. Fish
bowl pattern cut from
white copy paper.*

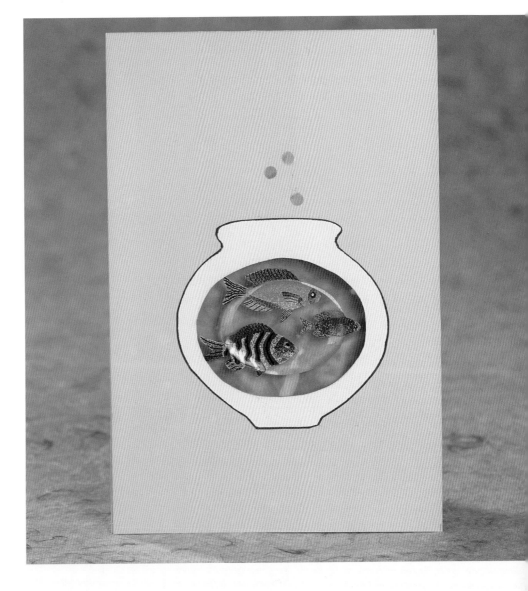

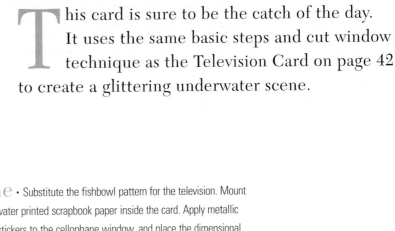

This card is sure to be the catch of the day. It uses the same basic steps and cut window technique as the Television Card on page 42 to create a glittering underwater scene.

one • Substitute the fishbowl pattern for the television. Mount the water printed scrapbook paper inside the card. Apply metallic fish stickers to the cellophane window, and place the dimensional oval sticker over the fish. Punch bubbles from the blue cardstock scraps and glue them above the fishbowl.

# chinese take-out

## MATERIALS

8" x 5½" (20cm x 14cm) brown cardstock, folded to a 4" x 5½" (10cm x 14cm) card

2½" x 3⅞" (6cm x 10cm) patterned origami paper

carton pattern pieces cut from white cardstock

4" (10cm) of 26-gauge steel wire

two flat wooden toothpicks

clear dimensional paint (TULIP Gellies)

embossing tool

1/16" (2mm) hole punch

tape

paper glue

scrapbook glue

basic tools (see page 8)

### MESSAGES

*Take Out, Good Eating!,
Let's Get Together*

Take out, anyone? This card is the perfect invitation to share a relaxed evening of Chinese food at home. An origami paper background sets the mood, over which the cut paper carton is assembled. The garnish is dimensional paint "rice," and handy toothpick "chopsticks" make this card simply irresistible.

one · Squeeze short dollops of dimensional paint to simulate rice over the top of the larger of the two cut carton pieces. See the pattern pn page 48 for exact placement. Allow the paint to dry completely before continuing.

two · Use a ruler and embossing tool to score the two marked lines on each carton piece.

three · Join the carton pieces together with scrapbook glue. Position the smaller piece over the right side of the larger piece. Fold the left-hand flap of the larger piece over the smaller piece. The rice will still be visible between the two open top flaps.

four · Punch a hole in the overlapping triangular corner on the left side of the carton. Thread one end of the wire through the hole. Shape the length of the wire into a square handle, and then tuck the other wire end behind the right side of the carton. Tape both wire ends flat against the backside of the carton.

 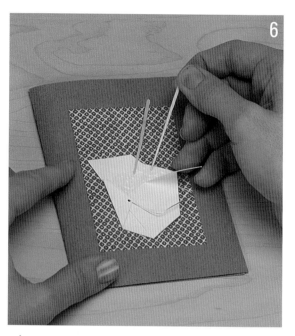

five · Apply paper glue to the back of the origami paper and mount it to the center of the card. Use scrapbook glue to position the box slightly above the bottom edge of the origami paper.

six · Use scrapbook glue to attach two toothpicks to the card. They should come out from the top of the rice-topped carton.

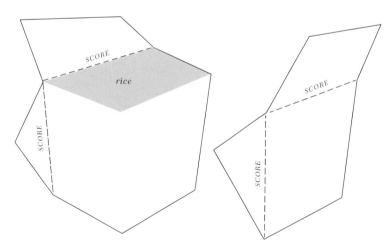

*Chinese take-out box cut from white cardstock. Patterns are full size.*

# fortune cookie card

## MATERIALS

8" x 5½" (20cm x 14cm) brown cardstock,
folded to a 4" x 5½" (10cm x 14cm) card

2½" x 3⅞" (6cm x 10cm) patterned
origami paper

top and bottom cookie (a, c, d) patterns
cut from tan cardstock

center cookie (b) pattern cut from
dotted tan cardstock

white copy paper fortune

computer and printer

paper glue

basic tools (see page 8)

### MESSAGES

*Good Fortune, True love lasts forever*

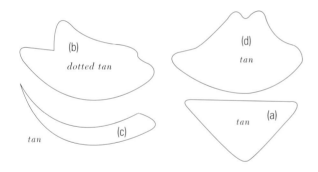

*Enlarge to 200%. Cookie pieces cut from cardstock.*

Take fate into your own hands and write a customized fortune on your computer using a 10pt Times New Roman font. Print it in red ink, trim and tuck it into this cookie of a card.

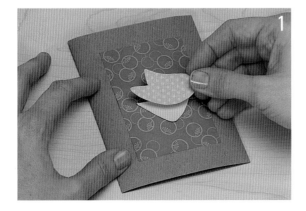

one · Start by mounting the origami paper to the center of the card. Glue the bottom fortune cookie pattern piece (a) just below the center of the origami paper. Glue the dotted middle pattern piece (b) over the top edge of the bottom cookie pattern piece.

two · Glue one end of the fortune over the middle pattern piece (b). Glue the small pattern piece (c) along the bottom edge of the top of the cookie (d). Glue the top of the cookie (c, d) over the top edge of the middle piece (b) trapping the fortune strip in place. Glue only the top of the cookie lid so that it can be lifted to reveal the fortune.

# victorian bird cage

## MATERIALS

3½" (9cm) circle of gold paper
for the cage

¼" (6mm) wide strip of gold paper

base pattern cut from black paper

tassel

bird, butterfly or flower stickers

plastic message stickers

paper glue

basic tools (see page 8)

## MESSAGES

*Love, Secret Garden, Forever*

*tip* > The closer and longer you cut the birdcage slits, the higher the birdcage will expand when opened. Be careful, it also becomes more prone to tearing!

Gently lift the tassel to reveal the beautiful birds and secret message inside. Based on early Valentine card designs, this technique still surprises and delights. Black paper contrasts with the colorful stickers, enhancing the impact when the hidden images appear.

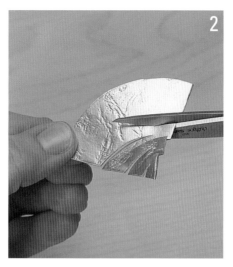

**one** · Glue the gold paper strip diagonally across the center of the black base pattern. Attach the bird stickers so that their feet stand on the gold paper strip. Apply the message sticker directly beneath the birds. It's important that both the images and message are closely grouped together in the center of the base so the cage will cover them.

**two** · To make the cage, fold the circle into four sections. Make alternating slits starting from one folded edge. Cut across the folded circle and stop just before you reach the opposite folded edge. Each cut will be increasingly larger as you work your way to the wider end. Be sure to leave ¼" (6mm) of paper at the top edge intact.

**three** · Slowly unfold the gold cage and spread it flat. Loop the center of the tassel through the smallest center cuts. Thread the tassel ends through the looped cord and gently pull them up to secure.

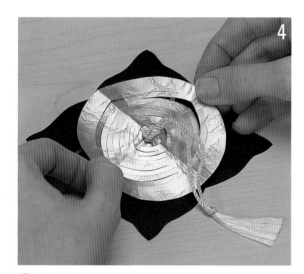

**four** · Working on the underside of the gold cage, apply glue to just the outside ¼" (6mm) edge of the cage. Flip the cage right side up and position it over the center of the base. Press the glued edge down. When the glue sets, lift the tassel to expand the cage. Your message will be visible through the gold paper slits.

*Base pattern cut from black paper. Pattern is full size.*

# party hats

## MATERIALS

2³⁄₈" x 12" (6cm x 30cm) strip, and a
1¹⁄₈"x 2¹⁄₈" (3cm x 5cm) rectangle
of white cardstock

two 2³⁄₈" x 1¾" (6cm x 4cm) rectangles
of blue foil cardstock for the front
and back card covers

hat pattern cut from metallic origami
paper, pink, purple, blue and green

12" (30cm) length of ¹⁄₈" (3mm) wide
black polka dot ribbon

raised plastic letters stickers

embossing tool

standard hole punch

paper glue

basic tools (see page 8)

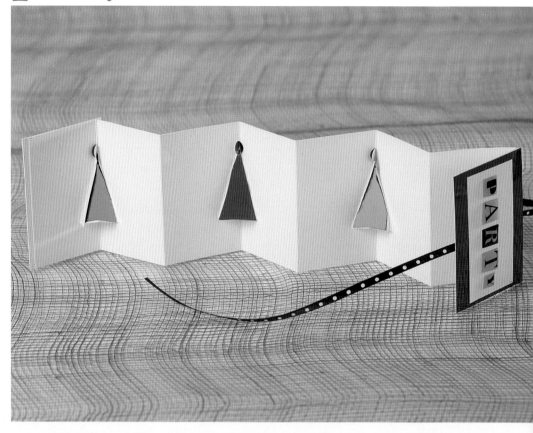

Good things often come in small packages. Send a
surprise in this whimsical card. When it's untied, it
unfurls into a length of sparkling party hats. The hats
are fitting for either a New Year or birthday celebration.

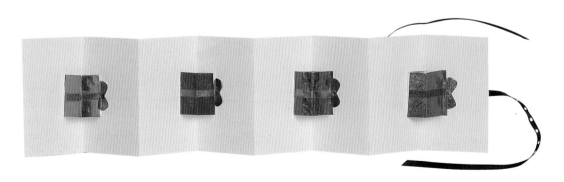

## ANOTHER SIMPLY BEAUTIFUL IDEA

The present card is made like the hats, except snip two ½" (1cm) slits in each fold,
position them 1" (3cm) apart. Fold the cut tabs up to make straight crease lines,
then unfold the paper strip. Push the underside of each rectangle up to reverse its
center fold. This will allow the presents to pop out. Decorate the packages with
the metallic paper and top the center of each bow with a paper-punched circle.

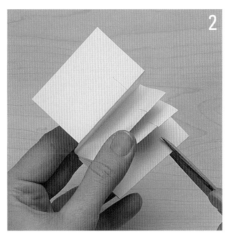

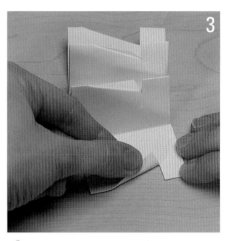

one • Use a ruler and embossing tool to score the cardstock strip at 1½" (4cm) intervals, making a total of seven score lines.

two • Accordion fold (see page 54) the cardstock strip along the score lines. With scissors snip a ¾" (2cm) slit across each fold. Position each slit ⅝" (2cm) from one edge of the paper. Make cuts on only one side of the strip.

three • Fold the paper over at each slit, so that you create a diagonal crease, then unfold so that an inverted v-shaped crease line remains above each slit.

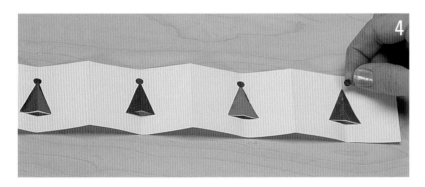

four • Glue a metallic paper hat pattern between each set of crease lines, aligning the bottom edge with the cut slit. Punch circles out of the metallic paper scraps and then glue one to the top of each triangle shaped hat. Push the underside of each hat up to reverse its center fold, so that it pops up when the card is unfolded.

five • Mount the white cardstock rectangle over one piece of blue foil and then apply letter stickers to the white cardstock. Glue the middle of the ribbon across the underside of the first page, and then glue the blue foil over the ribbon. Glue the other piece of blue foil under the last page of the paper strip. Once the glue has dried refold the paper strip, wrap the ribbon around the card and tie the ends in a bow.

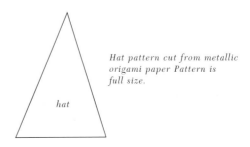

*Hat pattern cut from metallic origami paper Pattern is full size.*

hat

# what's cooking?

## MATERIALS

10" x 6⅝" (25cmx17cm) white cardstock, folded to a 5" x 6⅝" (13cmx17cm) card

10" x 6" (25cmx15cm) white copy paper

window pattern cut from blue paper

oven and sink patterns cut from black and white polka-dotted papers

wall pattern cut from yellow striped paper

oven door pattern cut from white scrapbook paper

6⅝" x 1¾" (17cm x 4cm) floor from orange patterned sticker sheet

window curtain pattern cut from orange patterned sticker sheet

cookie tray stickers

black felt-tip marker

paper glue

basic tools (see page 8)

*tip* > An accordion fold is basically a row of pleats of the same size. Fold lines facing down are called valleys, and fold lines facing up are called mountains.

Got the munchies? Check out this miniature kitchen and you'll find chocolate chip cookies baking in the oven. You don't need to know how to cook to assemble this vignette of domestic bliss. The only thing that's missing is the freshly baked cookie smell!

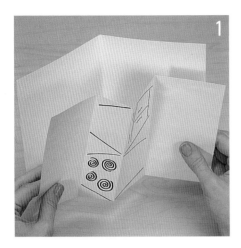

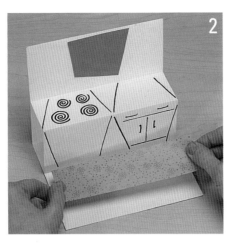

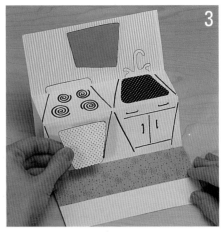

one · Draw the cabinet and stove lines in black marker onto the center of the white copy paper. The center fold should be at the 5" (13cm) mark. Use the pattern as your guide to make three fold lines, the first and last folds are valley folds, and the center fold is a mountain fold. Apply paper glue to the underside of the first and last folded flaps, then position the copy paper inside the card. Align the copy paper and card edges together, the center mountain fold section of the copy paper will remain unglued so that it pops forward when the card is opened.

two · Orient the card horizontally and then glue the blue paper window pattern centered over the stove and sink. Make sure the placement is correct with the wall pattern. Apply the floor sticker below the bottom edge of the oven and cabinet doors.

three · Edge the window opening and faucet with black marker. Glue the wall so the blue paper is below the window and the faucet above the sink. glue the sink beneath the faucet, then glue the oven below the stove top.

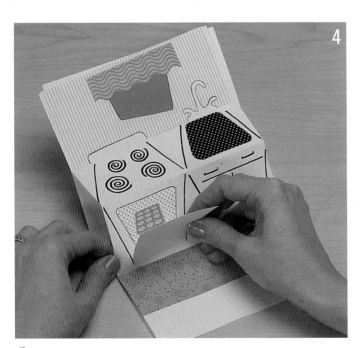

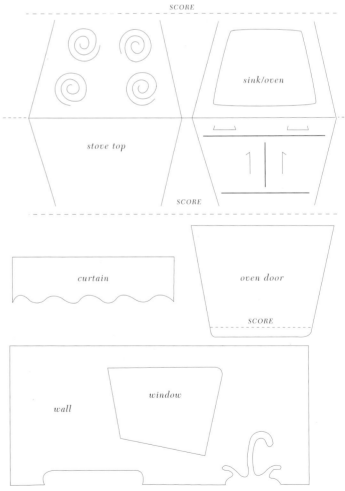

four · Apply the curtain sticker over the window and the cookie tray sticker in the oven. Score a line just above the base of the oven door pattern and glue this lower portion of the pattern under the oven.

*Enlarge to 200%. The counter cut from white copy paper, the wall from yellow scrapbook paper, with the window cut out, and the curtain from orange sticker paper The oven and sink from black and white polka-dotted papers. Cut the oven door from cardstock.*

55

# special event

**d**on't let the wonderful moments in life pass by without recognition. Take the time to make a unique card to celebrate each special event. As the years pass, these cards will become treasured keepsakes.

To congratulate a couple on their wedding day, choose between two beautiful wedding cards. One features an ornate wedding dress, and the second features a tempting three-tiered wedding cake. A simple pattern switch will alter the wedding cards and transform them into gorgeous anniversary cards. Once the couple has settled into family life, surprise the new parents with a delicate and darling baby card. The baby cards are made with soft tactile materials, making them simply irresistible to the touch.

Every new year brings a birthday. You can make them special by sending an interactive card. You'll find a puzzle card that's assembled to reveal the message. There's also a paper cake with a long shelf life and a card with a birthday pin for a special child in your life.

These original cards have been designed to surprise and delight. Find the perfect card to celebrate the special moments in your life.

**CHAPTER**

**2**

# the envelope, please

## MATERIALS

8" x 5½" (20cm x 14cm) white cardstock, folded to a 4" x 5½" (10cm x 14cm) card

envelope pattern cut from double-sided pink/blue cardstock paper

3⅛" x 4⅞" (8cm x 12cm) striped scrapbook paper

11" (28cm) length of ⅛" (3mm) white ribbon

message stamp and black stamp pad

embossing tool

paper glue

scrapbook glue

basic tools (see page 8)

### MESSAGES

*Best Wishes, Love, Forever, For You*

U ntie the bow and unfold the envelope to discover a secret message tucked inside. A sentiment presented so beautifully is sure to make an impression! This simple technique is fitting for almost any occasion— from a heartfelt thank you to a declaration of love.

**ANOTHER** SIMPLY **BEAUTIFUL** IDEA

**Change the paper color and the message to suit the sentiment! Use silver and gold for anniversaries, red and white for valentines and pastels for baby congratulations. You can use the pattern for any number of cards.**

one · Use an embossing tool and ruler to score four lines between the cut corners of the envelope pattern, creating a square in the center of the pattern. Stamp a message in the center of the pattern.

two · Apply paper glue to the underside of the striped paper rectangle. Then mount the rectangle to the center of the note card. Squeeze a small amount of scrapbook glue on the center of the striped paper. Place the middle of the ribbon over the glue. The ribbon ends will extend beyond the card.

three · Apply scrapbook glue to the underside of the stamped envelope. Glue only the center of the rectangle, and not the four flaps. Position the rectangle over the glued section of ribbon, then press it into place. Allow the glued layers of paper and ribbon to dry completely before proceeding.

four · To tie the envelope, first fold the side flaps over the center message. Next fold the bottom flap up, and finally fold the top flap down. Bring the ribbon ends together and tie them in a small bow. If necessary, trim the ribbon ends.

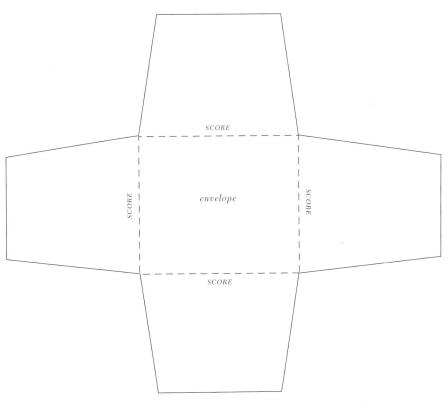

*Enlarge to 111%. Envelope pattern cut from two-sided cardstock.*

# chic paper purse

## MATERIALS

sheet of scrapbook paper

purse handle pattern cut from
blue cardstock

3" (8cm) long section of
green feathered boa

eyelet

mini brad

7" (18cm) silver elastic cord

¾" (2cm) circle punch

¹⁄₁₆" (2mm) and ⅛" (3mm) hole punches

eyelet setter and small hammer

craft knife

embossing tool

paper glue

scrapbook glue

basic tools (see page 8)

Make a fashion statement with this one-of-a-kind paper purse that has a sense of style all its own. Curvy, feathered and fun, this card is perfect for your personal correspondence. It's an excellent way to send party invitations as well. Small as an evening bag, it unbuttons for letter-sized writing.

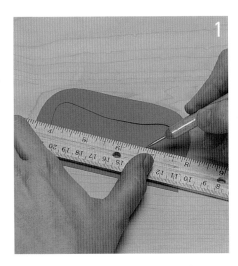

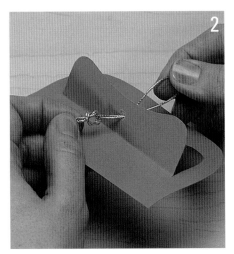

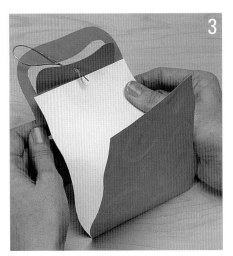

**one** · Use a craft knife to create the opening in the handle pattern, then use a ruler and embossing tool to score the base of the opening so it will fold over to make the front flap of the purse.

**two** · Punch a ⅛" (3mm) hole in the front flap of the handle, ⅜" (1cm) from the top edge. Thread an eyelet through the hole, then set it. Fold the elastic in half and thread both ends through the eyelet. Working under the purse flap, tie the ends together in an overhand knot. The resulting loop should be 1½" (4cm) long when unstretched.

**three** · Fold the scrapbook paper in half, with the patterned side out. Position the purse pattern along the fold line. Trace and cut out the purse through both layers of paper. Use paper glue to attach the top back of the purse over the handle base.

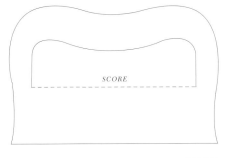

*SCORE*

*purse*

**four** · Apply a line of scrapbook glue along the underside edge of the purse handle flap and press the feathered boa into place. Punch a ¾" (2cm) circle out of blue paper for the clasp, then punch a ¹⁄₁₆" (2mm) hole in the center of the clasp. Thread the brad through the hole, and secure the brad to the front of the purse, 1½" (4cm) from the top. Close the feathered purse flap over the paper purse and stretch the loop over the clasp. If necessary, adjust the loop knot so that the paper purse lies flat.

*Enlarge to 200%. Purse pattern, and the purse handle pattern cut from blue cardstock.*

# good wishes

## MATERIALS

two 5½" (14cm) white cardstock squares

4½" x 4¼" (11cm x 11cm) yellow paper

3¾" x 3¼" (10cm x 8cm) patterned vellum

4½" (11cm) square envelope
(clear scrapbook envelope or cut a corner
from a larger cellophane envelope)

turquoise paper tag (or create your own
tag with a 1½" [4cm] circle punch)

metal message embellishment

6" (15cm) length of 1½" (4cm) ribbon

iridescent star confetti

two eyelets

eyelet setter and hammer

standard hole punch

⅛" (3mm) hole punch

embellishment glue

basic tools (see page 8)

## MESSAGES

*Love, Laugh, Wish*

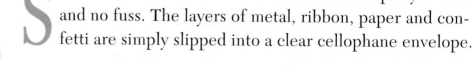

## ANOTHER SIMPLY BEAUTIFUL IDEA

Send a celebration! This card is its own little party— all fun and no fuss. The layers of metal, ribbon, paper and confetti are simply slipped into a clear cellophane envelope.

**For this card, I changed the message and used different colors. I also added a piece of origami mesh inside the package for added texture.**

one · Glue the center back of the metal message onto the paper tag.

two · If necessary, punch a hole in the top of the tag, just above the word. Lace ribbon through the tag and pull half the ribbon length through the hole.

three · Stack the vellum over the yellow paper, then place the tag and ribbon on the stacked papers. Insert the papers and tag into the open side of the clear envelope.

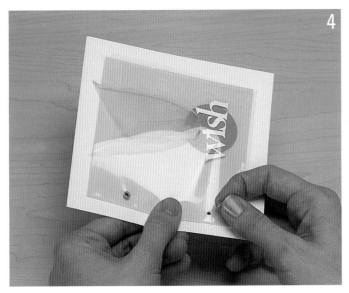

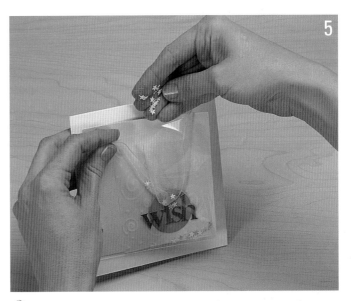

four · Score a fold line across each of the white cardstock pieces, 1" (3cm) from the left edge. Stack the scored cards together and position the open left edge of the envelope ½" (1cm) from the left edge of the white cards. Punch two ⅛" (3mm) holes through the envelope and the white cardstock. Position the holes ⅜" (1cm) from the left edge of the envelope and 1½" (4cm) from the top and bottom edges of the white cards. Set an eyelet into each hole to join the layers (the envelope, the yellow paper and the white cardstock) of the card together.

five · Sprinkle confetti into the top of the cellophane. If you like, secure the top of the cellophane closed with double-stick tape.

# little house card

## MATERIALS

7" x 5" (18cm x 13cm) blue cardstock, folded to a 3½" x 5" (9cm x 13cm) card

3½" x 2" (9cm x 5cm) green scrapbook paper for the grass

roof, chimney and steps patterns cut from black and white patterned scrapbook paper

house pattern cut from red patterned cardstock

house pattern cut from bold striped scrapbook paper

two cloud patterns cut from light blue scrapbook paper

red heart-shaped rhinestone

craft knife

embossing tool

⅛" (3mm) hole punch

paper glue

scrapbook glue

basic tools (see page 8)

## MESSAGES

*Congratulations on Your New Home,
Home is Where the Heart is*

The tiny windows and door of the little house card open to reveal different colored rooms. Tucked inside one is a shiny red heart. Whether you make the card to welcome new neighbors or send it to friends who have moved away, your thoughtfulness will be appreciated. It's a small step towards helping make their new house a home.

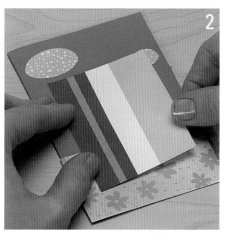

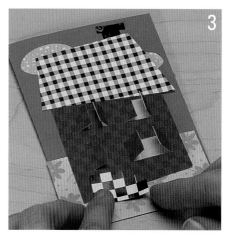

**one** · Use a craft knife to cut the marked window and door openings on the red cardstock house. Score the outside edges of the windows and door with an embossing tool and ruler. This will facilitate opening and closing the windows and door, and help keep the paper from tearing.

**two** · Use paper glue to attach all the cut paper pieces to the front of the card. Mount the grass on the bottom of the card and the two clouds at the top. Position the base of the striped inner house over the top of half of the grass.

**three** · On the underside of the red house, carefully apply glue between the cut windows and the door of the cardstock house, then position the outer house directly over the striped inner house. Mount the roof over the top of the house and tuck the base of the chimney under the top of the roof. Finally, mount the front steps under the doorway.

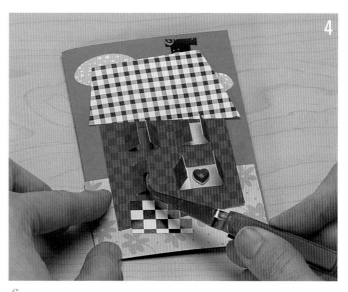

**four** · Use scrapbook glue to attach a rhinestone heart behind one of the windows. Punch a doorknob out of black scrap paper and glue it to the front door. Allow the glue under the rhinestone heart to set completely before mailing.

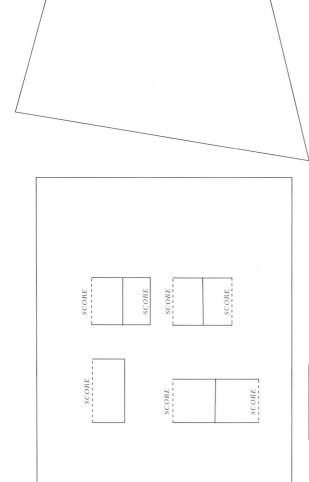

*The inner house cut from bold striped scrapbook paper, and the outer house red cardstock. The roof, chimney and steps cut from white and black scrapbook paper. The clouds cut light blue scrapbook paper. Pattern is full size.*

# wedding cake card

ANOTHER SIMPLY BEAUTIFUL IDEA

This tempting three-layered wedding cake was frosted with dimensional paint icing. Traditionally used on fabric, when used on paper the paint dries faster and creates an appealing raised surface for added textural appeal.

**Make a blooming wedding bouquet of white and vellum paper flowers. Squeeze a spiral of dimensional paint onto each flower center. After they dry, mount them in a cluster on a green vellum background. Tuck white cord stems under the flower heads, then slide the stems into a pink vellum bouquet.**

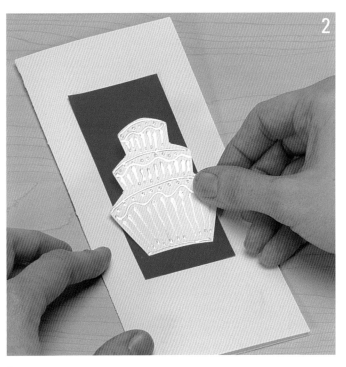

one · Trace the cake pattern on cardstock with a pencil. Squeeze a line of dimensional paint across the top of each of the three cake layers, then make a second wavy line under each straight line. Finally make a series of vertical stripes up from the base of each layer. Allow the painted lines to dry completely before cutting the cake out along the pencil lines.

two · Use double stick tape to attach the center of the red vellum background to the center of the white card, then glue the white cardstock cake to the center of the vellum.

*White cardstock cake and white vellum heart. Pattern is full size.*

three · Use double-stick tape to attach the vellum heart above the cake, then center a word sticker message at the bottom of the red vellum.

# wedding dress card

## MATERIALS

10¼" x 7¼" (26cm x 18cm) cream cardstock, folded to a 5⅛" x 7¼" (13cm x 18cm) card

3⅞" x 6⅛" (10cm x 16cm) tan cardstock

4⅛" x 6½" (10cm x 17cm) gold vellum

ruffle and dress skirt patterns cut from ivory heavyweight textured paper

bodice dress cut from ribbed off-white paper

ribbon rose

two pieces of 1¼" (3cm) long ⅛" (3mm) wide green ribbon

scrapbook glue

paper glue

hot glue and glue gun

basic tools (see page 8)

### MESSAGES

*Happy Anniversary, Here Comes the Bride, I Do, Eternal Love, Congratulations!*

ANOTHER SIMPLY BEAUTIFUL IDEA

**W**eddings and milestone anniversaries come once in a lifetime. Pair your most ornate decorative papers with silk flowers to make this elegant card. It's sure to be treasured as a memento of the day.

Like the first step of the dress card, mount the gold vellum and gold embossed cardstock over the front of the square card. Use paper glue to attach a heart to the center of the embossed card stock. Cut the ribbon flowers off the green ribbon and hot glue them over the heart. Because the flowers are bumpy, be sure to address the envelope before inserting the card.

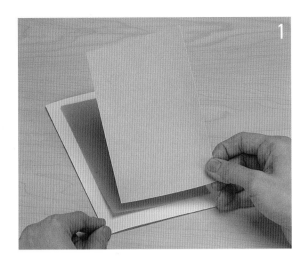

**one** · Paper glue the gold vellum over the center front of the cream card, then glue the tan cardstock centered over the vellum.

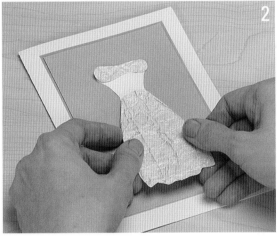

**two** · Use scrapbook glue to assemble the cut wedding dress pieces over the tan cardstock. First position the ribbed bodice towards the top, then attach the textured ruffle over the top edge of the bodice. Lay the top edge of the textured skirt over the bottom edge of the bodice.

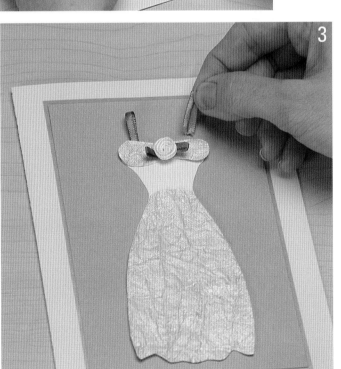

**three** · Hot glue the silk flower to the center of the bodice top. Fold each ribbon length in half and hot glue the ends under the bodice top to make the shoulder straps.

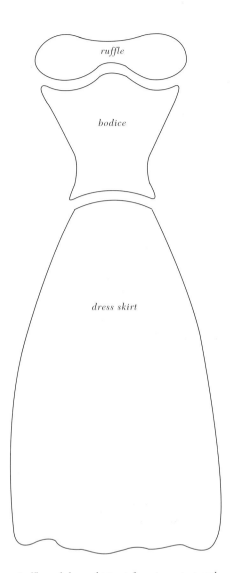

*ruffle*

*bodice*

*dress skirt*

*Ruffle and dress skirt cut from ivory textured paper. Bodice cut from ribbed off-white paper. Pattern is full size.*

*tip* > You can purchase ribbon roses two ways. They are sold by the yard stitched to a straight ribbon, or loose in cellophane packages. Locate them in the sewing notions department in fabric stores or with ribbons in the floral department of craft stores. They're available in different colors and sizes. Select the variety that works with your paper colors.

# make-a-wish

## MATERIALS

10¼" x 7" (26cm x 18cm) purple cardstock, folded to a 5⅛" x 7" (13cm x 18cm) card

⅞" (2cm) wide and 10" (25cm) long polka-dotted scrapbook paper

cake, plate and candle patterns cut from patterned adhesive sheets

two pieces of 2½" (6cm) long ¼" (6mm) wide pink ribbon

lower case alphabet stamps and black stamp pad

fine- and regular-tip black marker

blue and yellow felt markers

scrapbook glue

craft knife

basic tools (see page 8)

### MESSAGES

*Happy B day to You,
Make a Wish*

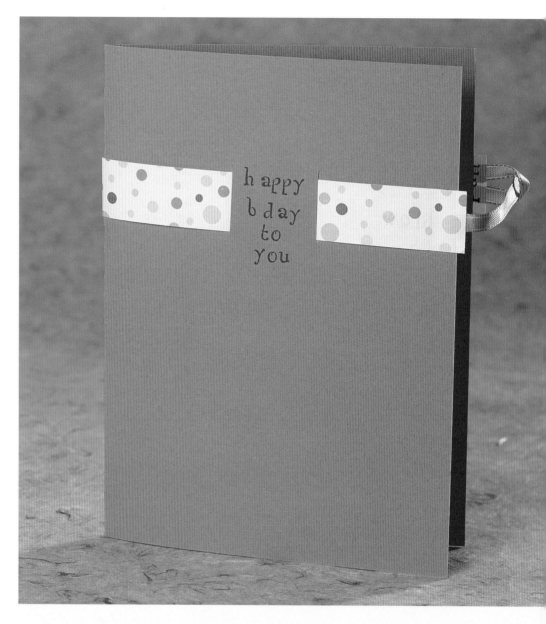

Get ready to make a wish! With a single pull of the paper strip you're guaranteed to blow out all the candles on this cake. The simple trick behind this engaging card is a sliding paper strip that weaves in and out through four slits in the card cover.

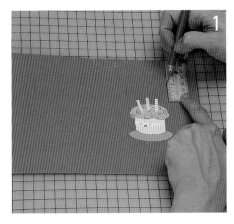
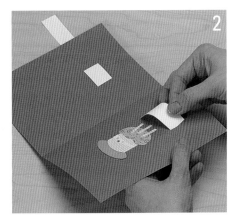
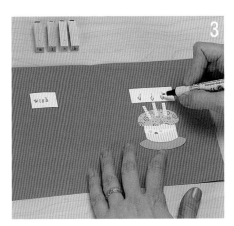

**one** · Inside the card, assemble the plate, cake and candle pattern pieces just below the center of the card. Use a craft knife to cut two vertical slits, 1" (3cm), above the cake. Position the left slit 1" (3cm) from the center fold, and the right slit 1" (3cm) from the right card edge. Make a second pair of 1" (3cm) long vertical slits on the inside front card cover. Position the right slit 2" (5cm) from the center fold, and the left slit 2" (5cm) from the left card edge.

**two** · Thread the paper strip through the slits, working from left to right. The back of the paper, which should be white, should show between the two pairs of slits, and the pattern should be visible on the outside of the card.

**three** · Adjust the paper strip so the ends are aligned with either side of the card. Use letter stamps to spell the word *wish* over the exposed paper on the left side of the card. Use yellow and black markers to draw candle flames above the cake candles on the right side of the card.

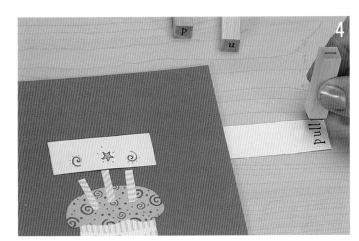
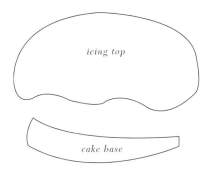
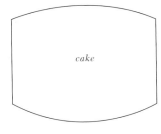

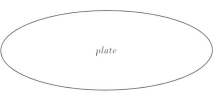

**four** · Gently pull the right paper end until both the *wish* message and candle flames are no longer showing. Stamp *blow* over the newly exposed paper on the left side, then use blue and black markers to draw alternating stars and spirals above the candles on the right side of the card. Stamp the word *pull* across the right end of the paper strip. Slide the decorated paper strip back into the card.

**five** · Close the card and stamp a message on the cardstock cover. Stack the words between the cut slits. Fold one of the ribbons in half and glue both ends under the *pull* end of the paper strip. Pinch the ribbon and paper together for a minute while the glue sets. Glue the other ribbon, unfolded, to the other end of the paper strip.

*icing top*

*cake base*

*cake*

*plate*

*candle*

*Birthday cake cut from a variety of patterned sticker papers. Pattern is full size.*

# birthday pin card

## MATERIALS

### PIN

shrink art sheets

pin back

large letter stamps

black pigment ink stamp pad

yellow paint marker

embellishment glue

### CARD

8½" x 5½" (22cm x 14cm) double-sided purple and orange cardstock, folded to a 4¼" x 5½" (11cm x 14cm) card

3" x 5" (8cm x 13cm) purple scrapbook paper

star pattern cut from red glitter cardstock

decorative scallop-edged scissors

craft knife

paper glue

basic tools (see page 8)

**ANOTHER** SIMPLY
BEAUTIFUL
IDEA

P resent and card, all in one! The message on the front cover is actually a shrink plastic pin. It slips easily off the card and can be worn by the birthday boy or girl. Everyone will know it's his or her special day.

**You can use a pin card for more than just birthdays! Change the text on the pin to suit the occasion. Choose a background that follows the theme, such as balloons.**

72

**one** · Use large letter stamps and solvent ink to stamp a message onto a piece of shrink plastic. Cut out the message, leaving some white plastic around the stamped letters. Edge the cut plastic with yellow paint marker.

**two** · Shrink the plastic according to the package instructions. Let it cool, then use embellishment glue to attach the pin back to the back of the plastic. Set the finished pin aside while the glue sets.

**three** · Orient the card vertically and use decorative scissors to trim ¼" (6mm) off the right edge of the card cover. This will reveal the orange side of the cardstock inside the card. Use paper glue to mount the purple paper down the front of the card. Then attach the star pattern over the purple paper.

**four** · Unfold the card and lay it over a protected work surface. Use a craft knife to make a horizontal cut across the center of the star. Make small vertical cuts at either end of the horizontal cut. The center of this cut should be long enough to accommodate the pin back.

*Enlarge to 125%. Star pattern cut from red glitter cardstock.*

**five** · Refold the card and press the pin back into the cut slit. Place a piece of bubble wrap or corrugated cardboard inside the card before mailing. This will keep the pin back from puncturing the inside of the card.

# pretty paper cake

## MATERIALS

1½" x 10" (4cm x 25cm) cake strip cut from pink patterned cardstock

3¾" (10cm) circle cut from scrapbook paper for the small plate

4" (10cm) circle cut from purple cardstock for the large plate

icing patterns cut from yellow, purple and light pink cardstock

10" (25cm) length of ⅛" (3mm) ribbon

adhesive candle embellishments

alphabet stamps and purple stamp pad

spiral punch

star hand punch

⅛" (3mm) hole punch

embossing tool

paper glue

basic tools (see page 8)

A long shelf life and zero calories are only two of the winning features of this paper cake card. It's mailed flat, but in an instant the three separate pieces quickly assemble into a gorgeous, three-dimensional cake.

**one** • Use the alphabet letter stamps to stamp the message *Happy Birthday to You* across the patterned side of the cake strip. Allow the ink to dry before continuing.

**two** • Flip the cake strip over and score the underside at 1" (3cm) intervals, for a total of nine score lines. Turn the scored strip right side up and bring the strip ends together and punch a hole through both layers. Thread the ribbon through the holes to connect the strip into a cylinder shape. Tie the ribbon ends into a loose bow so that the cylinder can fold flat for mailing.

**three** • Glue the smaller plate over the center of the larger plate. Glue the three layers of frosting together. Stack them largest to smallest. Sprinkle the top yellow layer of frosting with punched paper spirals and stars, then glue them in place.

**four** • Assemble the cake by placing the cylinder cake strip onto the plate and laying frosting on top. You'll need to use two adhesive candle embellishments to make each candle around the top of the cake. Position the candles in the open areas between the frosting bumps. Trap the top edge of the paper cake in the adhesive between the candle pairs.

**five** • To mail the cake, remove the frosting, flatten the cake strip by folding it in half, then stack the three pieces together and slip them into an envelope.

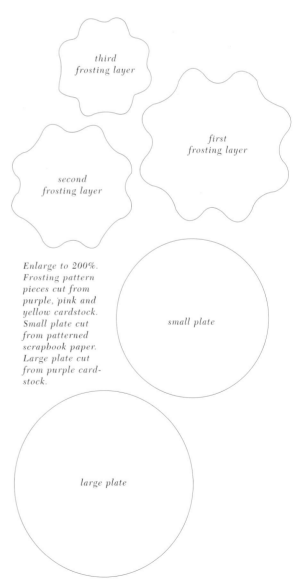

*third frosting layer*

*first frosting layer*

*second frosting layer*

*Enlarge to 200%. Frosting pattern pieces cut from purple, pink and yellow cardstock. Small plate cut from patterned scrapbook paper. Large plate cut from purple cardstock.*

*small plate*

*large plate*

# little feet

## MATERIALS

7" x 5" (18cm x 13cm) white cardstock, folded to a 3½" x 5" (9cm x 13cm) card

2¼" x 3¾" (6cm x 10cm) light blue suede paper

1⅞" x 2½" (5cmx6cm) rectangle of light blue vellum

baby feet scrapbook embellishment (substitute a footprint embossing plate)

small safety pin

woven label

embossing tool

scrapbook glue

basic tools (see page 8)

### MESSAGES

*Pitter patter, Little One*

W ho can resist adorable baby fingers and toes? Delicate footprints are embossed onto vellum and then safety-pinned to the front of the card. Once you've purchased a metal rubbing or embossing plate you can use it to make countless cards for baby announcements, shower invitations and thank-you notes.

**ANOTHER** SIMPLY **BEAUTIFUL** IDEA

Pretty in pink, this handprint card is the perfect congratulations for a baby girl. The woven labels add to the softness of the finished card. Find them where scrapbook embellishments are sold.

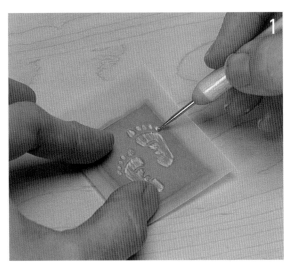

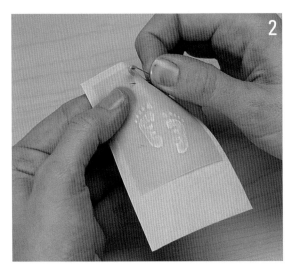

one · Lay the bottom of the vellum rectangle over the metal plate. If you're using an embossing plate, lay it over the bottom of the vellum rectangle. Gently rub the embossing tool over the indentations in the plate, or in the openings of the embossing plate. Where the vellum has been pushed into a relief it should discolor and appear white.

two · Use a safety pin to attach the top of the embossed vellum ⅛" (3mm) down from the top of the blue suede rectangle.

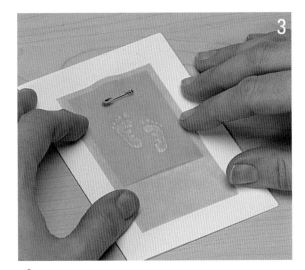

three · Glue the suede paper to the center of the front of the white card.

four · Glue the woven label message to the bottom of the blue suede beneath the vellum.

# baby buggy card

## MATERIALS

8" x 5½" (20cm x 14cm) white cardstock, folded to a card 4" x 5½" (10cm x 14cm)

3" x 3" (8cm x 8cm) yellow handmade paper

buggy pattern pieces cut from white suede paper

1" (3cm) and ½" (1cm) white plastic buttons

2½" (6cm) length of yellow baby ricrac

6½" (17cm) length of 24-gauge white wire

word stamp and black stamp pad

roundnose pliers

scrapbook glue

basic tools (see page 8)

### MESSAGES

*Congratulations!, New Baby!, It's a Boy/Girl!, Welcome to the World*

Simple and sweet. This charming card will delight new parents, and most likely be cherished in a baby's scrapbook. Assembling the pattern is simple. It's the mixture of materials— buttons, ricrac, suede and handmade paper— that make the card special.

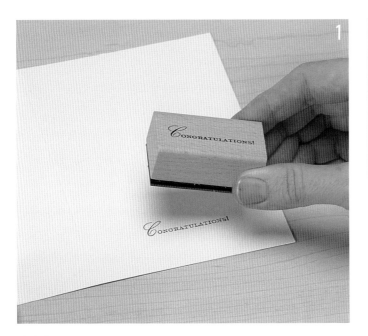

one • Stamp the message near the bottom of the card cover.

two • Glue the yellow handmade paper square above the stamped message. Cut the buggy patterns from page 80 out of white suede paper.

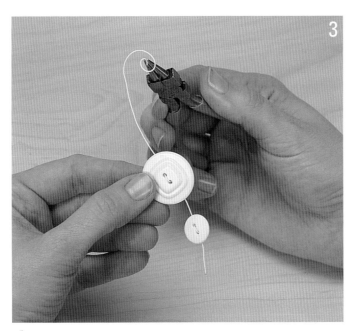

three • Connect the buggy wheels by threading the small and large buttons on the wire length. Bend the short end of the wire above the small button and the long end of the wire above the large button. Use roundnose pliers to shape the long wire end into a spiral buggy handle.

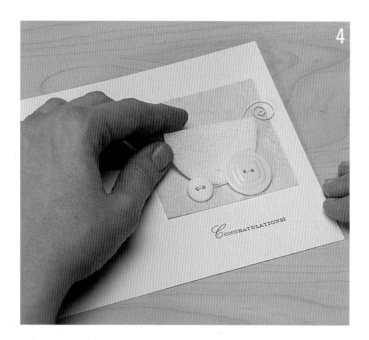

**four** · Apply a generous amount of glue to the underside of the button wheels and position them at the bottom of the yellow background. Glue the larger buggy piece just under the top of the buttons to cover the short wire end and the connection between the wheels.

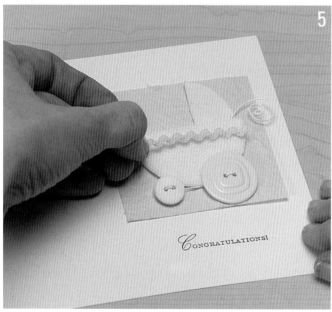

**five** · Glue the top of the buggy alongside the spiraled handle. Glue the ricrac just under the top edge of the larger buggy piece. Allow the glue under the button wheels to set completely before mailing.

*tip* > Try using different textured white paper for each part of the buggy. This will add visual interest to your card.

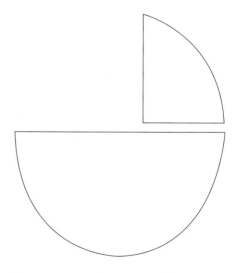

*Buggy patterns cut from white suede paper. Pattern is full size.*

# baby bib card

## MATERIALS

8" x 5½" (20cm x 14cm) white cardstock, folded to a 4" x 5½" (10cm x 14cm) card

2¾" x 3" (7cm x 8cm) pink handmade paper

bib pattern cut from white suede paper

pink rabbit button

clear round button

pink baby ricrac

word stamp and black stamp pad

scrapbook glue

basic tools (see page 8)

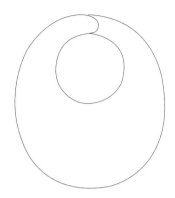

*Enlarge to 125%. Bib pattern cut from white suede paper.*

This card isn't just for little girls. A simple switch to blue buttons, ricrac and handmade paper and you can create a card for a bouncing baby boy.

one • As with the Baby Buggy card on page 78, first stamp the message, then glue the pink handmade paper square above it. Glue the bib to the center of the pink handmade paper.

two • Glue the rabbit button on the front of the bib, and the small button over the cut at the back of the bib's neck. Glue pink ricrac around the outside edge of the bib and trim away the excess. Allow the glue under the buttons to set completely before mailing.

81

# flower power card

Brighten someone's day with this surprising flower that is a beautiful card. The vibrant flower instantly blooms when it's pulled from the envelope. Sending flowers has never been so easy or affordable.

one · Fold each square in half diagonally, then in half twice more, for a total of three separate folds. Center a matching sized petal pattern between the folded edges of each piece. Trace and cut the double petal shape from the top open edge. Unfold to reveal a cut flower.

two · Working largest to smallest, stack and glue the four flower centers together. Rotate each flower clockwise so the petals alternate.

three · Print a message from your computer onto orange paper. Apply a dimensional sticker over the message. Cut along the edge of the plastic sticker. Glue the message button to the center of the flower.

four · Use the pattern to cut out the leaves from green paper, then fold along the center. Glue the folded leaves to the center back of the flower. The leaf tips should extend about ½" (1cm) above the petals.

five · Working from the inside to the outside, fold each petal down over the center button. Continue circling around the flower clockwise until all the petals are folded down. Hold the petals down with one hand while you slip the finished card into an addressed envelope. Position the leaf tips so they face out to make a convenient finger hold for the recipient to pull out the card.

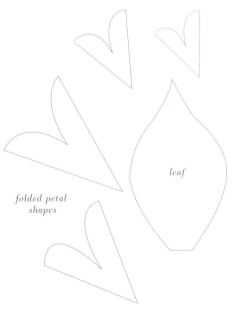

*folded petal shapes*

*leaf*

*Enlarge to 200%. Three petal patterns cut from colored copy paper. Leaf pattern cut from green copy paper.*

# catch a falling star

## MATERIALS

8" x 5½" (20cm x 14cm) white cardstock, folded to a 4" x 5½" (10cm x 14cm) card

4" x 5½" (10cm x 14cm) double-sided blue cardstock

scraps of double-sided blue cardstock

two clear star rhinestones

sewing needle and blue thread

star paper punch

awl

craft knife

tape

paper glue

embellishment glue

basic tools (see page 8)

Know someone who stands out from the crowd? Make this card to show them how brightly they shine. The rhinestone star and smaller punched paper stars twirl on sewn threads across a cut paper window.

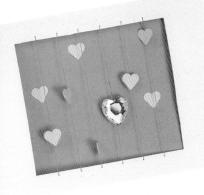

ANOTHER SIMPLY BEAUTIFUL IDEA

**Pull someone's heartstrings with this beautiful card. This card is assembled like the star card except for a few minor changes. First orient the card horizontally and stitch with pink thread. Glue a light pink background inside the card and dark pink punched paper hearts onto the threads. Finally, use heart-shaped rhinestones instead of star-shaped ones.**

one · Use a craft knife to cut a 3½" x 3" (9cm x 8cm) rectangular window in the front of the card. Orient the card vertically and use an awl to punch matching pairs of holes every ½" (1cm) along the top and bottom of the window. To help prevent tears, position the holes ⅛" (3mm) in from the window edge.

two · Bring the threaded needle from inside the card out to the front. Draw the length of the thread through the hole, stopping to tape the end inside the card. Stitch across the opening and poke the needle through the matching hole on the opposite side of the card. Inside the card, stitch across to the next hole. Bring the needle out this hole to make a second stitch across the front opening. Continue working in this fashion, always making horizontal stitches inside the card and vertical stitches on the outside. When you've finished connecting all the punched holes, remove the needle, trim the thread and tape it to the inside of the card.

three · Punch stars out of the paper scraps. Glue two stars with the dark sides together, trapping one of the threads between them. Glue a pair of stars to each of the remaining threads staggering them at different heights.

four · Glue the dark blue side of the paper inside the card. Glue light blue stars onto the blue paper, positioning them in empty areas beneath the threads.

five · Apply embellishment glue to the back of one of the rhinestone stars. Hold it, glue side up, under one of the threads. Press the back of a second rhinestone into the glue, trapping the thread between the two rhinestones. Allow the glue to dry completely before standing the card upright.

# puzzle card

## MATERIALS

blank puzzle card (Puzzle Gram)

torn red, blue, yellow, purple, orange and white tissue paper pieces

découpage medium and brush

alphabet letter stickers

metallic star stickers

craft knife

basic tools (see page 8)

## MESSAGES

*Happy Birthday to You,
Best Wishes, Congratulations!*

Decoding the hidden message is half the fun with this card. Assemble the puzzle to unscramble the message. This interactive card is perfect for anyone who's young at heart. Découpage instantly transforms the blank puzzle into a piece of art. You'll need plenty of time for the card to dry, so plan to make this card a couple of days before it needs to be mailed.

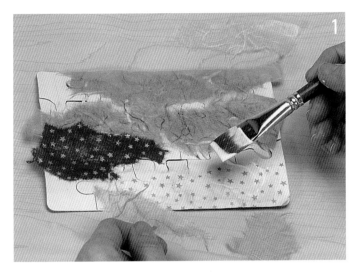

**one** · Working over a protected surface, apply a thin coat of découpage medium over the puzzle, then lay torn tissue paper pieces into the glue. When the puzzle is covered in tissue paper, apply a thin second coat of the découpage medium over the surface. Be careful; too much glue or tissue paper will make separating the puzzle pieces in step 3 more difficult. Allow the glue to dry completely before continuing. If necessary, place the dried puzzle under heavy books to flatten.

**two** · Once the puzzle is dry and flat, apply letter stickers to create a message across the puzzle pieces. Decorate around the lettering with star stickers. Trim away any tissue paper that hangs over the edges.

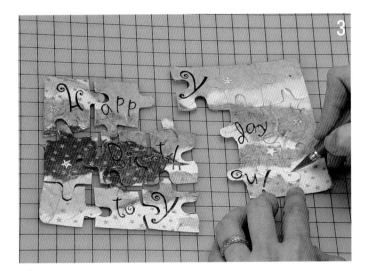

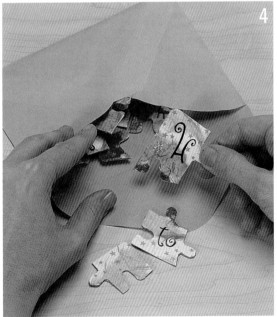

**three** · With a craft knife, carefully cut along the stamped puzzle lines to separate the pieces. It may be necessary to flip the puzzle over and cut along the underside of the lines.

**four** · Mail the separated puzzle pieces in a sturdy envelope. If necessary, line the envelope with cardstock to protect the puzzle pieces.

# crazy cat

## MATERIALS

10¾" x 4¼" (27cm x 11cm) piece of pink patterned cardstock

cat body pattern cut from grey cardstock

cat head cut from grey patterned cardstock

two tiny black rhinestones for the eyes

small black rhinestone for the nose

two 1½" (4cm) lengths of black thread for the whiskers

fine-tip black marker

embossing tool

scrapbook glue

paper glue

basic tools (see page 8)

## MESSAGES

*Hey Cool Cat, What's Up?, Happy Birthday, Doggone Fun*

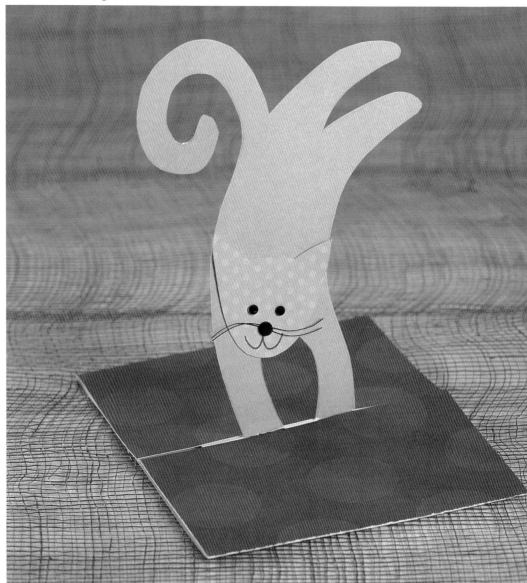

ANOTHER SIMPLY BEAUTIFUL IDEA

This pet does tricks and begs to be displayed. The cat flips upright after it's pulled from the envelope. The front half of the brightly patterned base opens so you can write a message on the white paper inside.

The dog card is assembled just like the cat. Simply use the pattern on page 88 and switch cardstock colors. Cut the base from purple and the head and body from tan and brown cardstock. Skip the whiskers. For personality, add a color spot under the pooch's eye and to the tip of his tail.

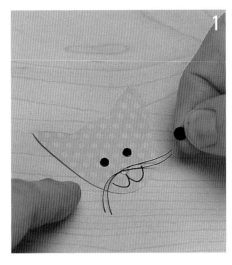

**one** · With a felt-tip marker draw a rounded *w*-shaped mouth at the base of the head. Use scrapbook glue to attach two tiny rhinestone eyes halfway down the head. Apply another dot of glue to the tip of the middle mouth line. Place the center of two black whisker threads in the glue and trap them in place with the rhinestone nose.

**two** · Use paper glue to mount the head above the front legs of the body pattern.

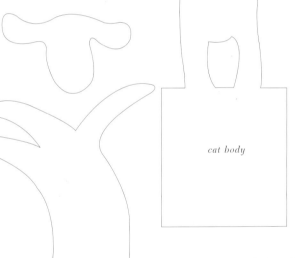

**three** · Use a ruler and embossing tool to make score lines on the pink cardstock, 2⅝" (7cm) from one end and 2⅝" (7cm) from the other end. Fold the resulting flaps towards the center to form the card base. Use paper glue to attach the tab end of the cat under the back flap, then fold the cat's body upright at the base of its front paws. Write a message under the front flap.

*cat body*

*dog body*

*Enlarge to 200%. Cat body and head pattern cut from tan cardstock. Dog variation body pattern cut from dark brown and head cut from tan cardstock.*

# seasonal and holiday

a playful twist on standard holiday greetings, these original card designs are sure to stand out from the crowd of their manufactured counterparts. December is one of the busiest times for sending cards, and I've included a number of quick and clever designs that won't slow you down. Revel in the beauty of the season and make winter cards that feature a frosted snowflake or a winter woodland scene. These cards are appropriate for everyone on your list.

You'll find cards for the warm weather holidays as well. Sometimes the arrival of an unexpected card makes even more of an impact. The bikini and Hawaiian shirt cards are sure to pass along the excitement of a tropical escape. Whatever the destination, the vacation cards excellent way to wish friends bon voyage.

As the weather cools and the days grow shorter, don't let your mood grow somber.

Be creative with zany Halloween cards. The images are fun, not scary, and the playful components appeal to the child in all of us. Before the first snowflakes fly, savor the last vestiges of fall and send leaf notes with messages of thanksgiving.

Open the pages of this section to find a card appropriate for every time of the year.

**CHAPTER**

**3**

# hearts

## MATERIALS

8½" x 5½" (22cm x 14cm) dark red
cardstock, folded to a 4¼" x 5½"
(11cm x 14cm) card

black and white patterned scrapbook
paper (gingham, love-themed type,
vintage floral and floral striped)

two 10" (25cm) long and ¼" (1cm) wide
red ribbon

scrapbook glue

basic tools (see page 8)

P ledge your eternal love with this card. The deep red card
is the perfect backdrop for the chain of black and white
paper hearts. Tie the red ribbon in a bow before sending
the card. When it's untied and opened, the center hearts will
pop forward.

**one** • Make a chain of hearts by tracing the heart pattern four times, side-by-side, on two strips of of the black and white floral paper. Cut out the two chains of four connected hearts. Cut two individual heart patterns from each of the three remaining patterned papers, for a total of six hearts. Glue three of these individual hearts over the hearts on each paper strip, one of the floral hearts on each strip will remain uncovered.

**two** • Apply paper glue to the underside of one of the finished heart strips and then position it across the center of the front and back covers of the unfolded card.

**three** • Accordion fold the second heart strip, and apply glue to the under-sides of the first and last hearts on the strip.

*Heart cut from black and white patterned scrapbook paper. Pattern is full size.*

**four** • Working inside the card, position the first and last glued hearts to the right and left card edges. Make sure they're aligned with the hearts on the card cover. Before pressing the hearts in place slip one end of a ribbon under each heart so that it's sandwiched between the paper and card. The two center hearts remain unglued so that they'll pop forward when the card is opened. After the glue has dried, tie the ribbon ends into a bow before placing the finished card in an envelope.

# candy heart

## MATERIALS

8" x 9¼" (20cm x 24cm) striped scrapbook paper, folded to a 4" x 9¼" (10cm x 24cm) card

4" x 9¼" (10cm x 24cm) white dotted pink cardstock

4" x 9¼" (10cm x 24cm) pink vellum

pastel yellow copy paper

craft knife

computer and printer

paper glue

double-stick tape

basic tools (see page 8)

## MESSAGES

*Be Mine, 4-Ever, Hugs, Kisses*

ANOTHER SIMPLY BEAUTIFUL IDEA

Perfect for your sweetheart, this valentine message will melt hearts all year long. The paper color and sentiments are both inspired by the classic conversational heart candies.

If you have trouble selecting just one candy message, go ahead and print more on different colored papers. These additional hearts can be mounted alongside the heart window, inside the card or even on the envelope.

*Heart pattern. Pattern is full size.*

one • Trace the heart pattern on the front of the card. Working on a protected surface, cut along the traced lines with a craft knife to make a heart-shaped opening.

two • Working inside the card, use double stick tape to attach the vellum sheet to the inside front cover. The vellum will create a semi-transparent pink heart-shaped window. Glue the dotted pink cardstock opposite the vellum to strengthen the card.

three • Print your message with red ink on yellow copy paper. Center the heart pattern over the printed message and trace around the heart with pencil. Cut the heart-shaped message out and glue it inside the card so that it's visible through the pink window when the card is closed.

# snapshot

## MATERIALS

Black cardstock for the camera

Travel printed scrapbook paper for the inside of the card

brown cardstock scraps

¾" x 5" (2cm x 13cm) strip of white and black patterned scrapbook paper

1¼" x ¾" (3cm x 2cm) rectangle of silver holographic sticker sheet

1¼" (3cm) metal rimmed tag (with the wire loop removed)

travel stickers

11" (28cm) gold cord

1⁄16" (.2mm) paper punch

paper glue

scrapbook glue

basic tools (see page 8)

## MESSAGES

Bon Voyage, Off We Go!, Vacation

Say cheese! This classic little black camera is sure to build excitement for an upcoming vacation. It's also a helpful reminder to pack camera and film for the trip. There's plenty of room on the folded page inside to write a short note and set a date to share vacation pictures.

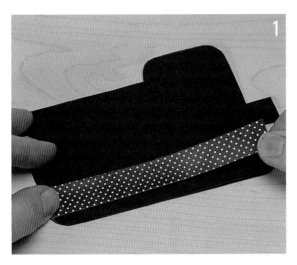

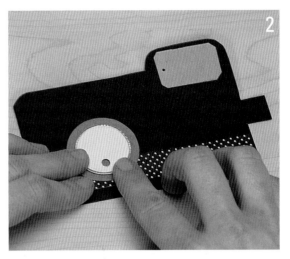

one · Fold a piece of black cardstock in half. Position the camera pattern against the folded edge of the cardstock. Trace and cut the camera out from both layers of paper, leaving the fold uncut. Trim the extended tab from the front of the card. To begin decorating the front of the card, use paper glue to attach the black and white patterned strip across the lower half of the camera.

two · Cut both a 1½" (4cm) circle and the flash pattern out of brown cardstock scraps. Use scrapbook glue to attach the circle on the left side of the camera, overlapping the top edge of the patterned strip. Attach the flash to the raised right corner. Use scrapbook glue to attach the metal rimmed tag lens to the center of the circle.

three · Apply a circular travel sticker over the tag lens and a message sticker above it. Center the holographic sticker inside the brown flash.

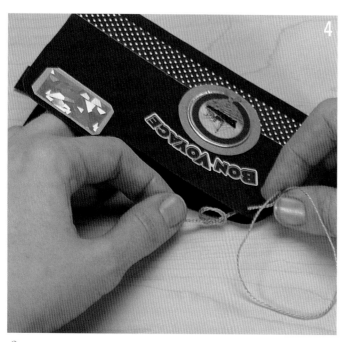

four · Punch a hole through the left corner of the front of the camera. Fold the gold cord in half and thread both ends through the front of the card. Tie them together in an overhand knot that will rest inside the card.

five · Fold the travel paper in half with the printed side out, then position the camera pattern against the fold. Trace and cut the pattern out through both layers of paper, omitting the raised flash and tab. Slip it inside the finished camera. This will give you white inner pages to write your message. Close the card by folding the black tab over the front of the card before placing it in the envelope.

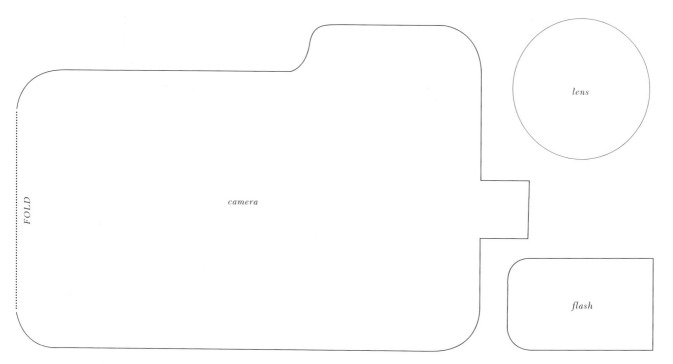

*FOLD*

*camera*

*lens*

*flash*

*Camera patterns cut from black cardstock and travel paper. Lens and flash cut from brown cardstock. Patterns are full size.*

# carry-on

## MATERIALS

brown cardstock for the suitcase

map printed scrapbook paper for the inside of the card

luggage tag cut from red cardstock

travel stickers

2½" (6cm) gold cord

9" (23cm) long section of ⅛" (3mm) wide black ribbon

1⁄16" (.2mm) hole punch

craft knife

basic tools (see page 8)

one · Fold the brown cardstock in half, then cut out a suitcase shape against the fold. Working on a protected surface, use a craft knife to remove the interior portion of the handle.

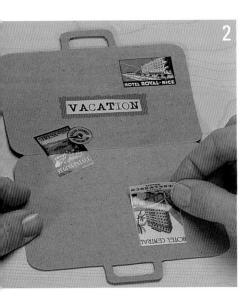

two · Open the card and apply travel stickers to the outside of the suitcase. Overlap some of the smaller stickers together and place a larger message sticker across the front of the suitcase.

three · Fold the map paper printed side out. Line the suitcase pattern against the fold, then trace and cut through both layers of paper, this time omitting the handles. Place the map papers inside the suitcase. Punch a hole in the red label and thread a 2½" (6cm) cord through the hole and around one suitcase handle and knot the ends. Tie the suitcase handles closed with black ribbon.

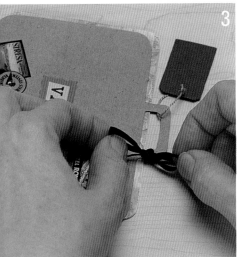

If you can't squeeze into their suitcase, at least you can send your travelling friends good wishes with this card.

*Enlarge to 200%. Suitcase pattern cut from brown cardstock.*

FOLD

# tropical escape

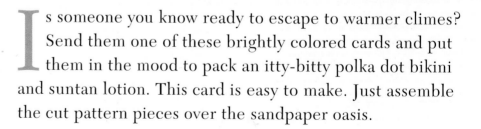

## MATERIALS

8" x 5½" (20cm x 14cm) purple cardstock, folded to a 4" x 5½" (10cm x 14cm) card

2⅛" x 4" (5cm x 10cm) textured yellow paper

2" x 3½" (5cm x 9cm) medium grit sandpaper

bikini pattern cut from purple polka-dotted scrapbook paper

light purple paper scrap

24-gauge purple wire

gold seed bead

fine-tip black marker

roundnose pliers

paper glue

scrapbook glue

basic tools (see page 8)

## MESSAGES

*Hit the Beach, Relax*

Is someone you know ready to escape to warmer climes? Send them one of these brightly colored cards and put them in the mood to pack an itty-bitty polka dot bikini and suntan lotion. This card is easy to make. Just assemble the cut pattern pieces over the sandpaper oasis.

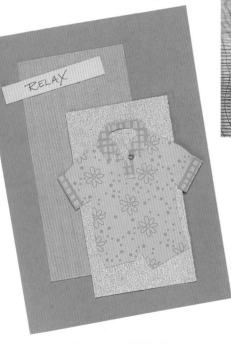

ANOTHER SIMPLY BEAUTIFUL IDEA

If a Hawaiian shirt better suits your recipient's sense of style, simply switch colors and cut out a shirt from the patterns found on page 115 to make this card. It's easier than the bikini card. Skip the wire-shaping step completely and use the seed bead for a shirt button.

**one** · Use paper glue to attach the textured yellow paper to the lower right corner of the purple card. Use scrapbook glue to mount the sandpaper over the top left corner of the yellow paper.

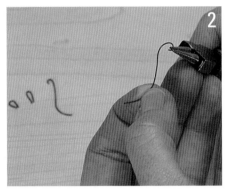

**two** · Use roundnose pliers to fold two ½" (1cm) long pieces of wire in half to make two small hip ties. To shape the neck ties, spiral one end of a 1½" (4cm) long wire, then spiral one end of a 1" (3cm) long piece of wire.

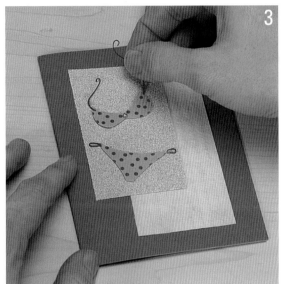

**three** · Use scrapbook glue to attach the two-piece bikini to the sandpaper. Next glue the hip ties to the bikini bottom and the neck ties to the bikini top. Finally glue a small metal seed bead to the center of the bikini top.

*bikini*

*Bikini patterns cut from purple polka dot scrapbook paper. Hawaiian shirt variation cut from patterned scrapbook paper. Patterns are full size.*

**four** · Write a message on a light purple scrap of paper and glue it over the yellow paper at the bottom right hand side of the card. Allow the glued wire pieces and bead to dry completely before mailing.

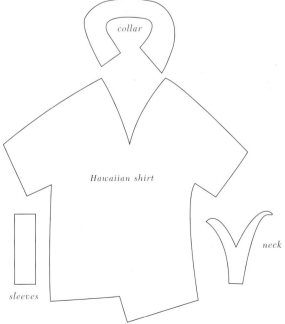

*collar*

*Hawaiian shirt*

*neck*

*sleeves*

# gone fishin'

## MATERIALS

8½" x 8" (22cm x 20cm) white cardstock, cut and folded to a 8½" x 4" (22cm x 10cm) card

4" x 8½" (10cm x 22cm) piece of scrapbook paper with a water pattern

2½" x 8½" (6cm x 22cm) hemlock patterned vellum

fishing pole and handle patterns cut from a simulated wood grain sticker sheet

black paper scrap

18" (46cm) length 32-gauge silver wire

20" (51cm) length of blue thread

fish sticker

⅝" (2cm) and ¹⁄₁₆" (2mm) circle punch

mini brad

awl

paper glue

double stick tape

basic tools (see page 8)

### MESSAGES

*To Dad, Happy Father's Day, Gone Fishin*

C atch them hook, line and sinker. . . this card will be a reeling success with the fishermen in your life! The rod is strung with a thread line that passes through to the inside of the card to catch a realistic-looking fish sticker.

*tip* > Rely on patterned scrapbook papers and stickers to add impact to your cards. Solid blue paper wouldn't be nearly as eye-catching as the simulated water. The same is true of the wood grain fishing rod and the detailed fish sticker.

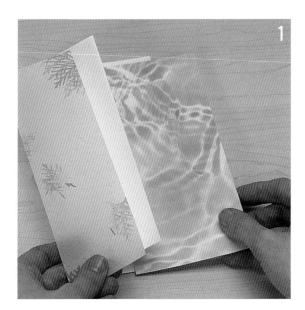

one · Trim 1½" (4cm) from the edge of the card cover. Use double-stick tape to attach the vellum sheet over the trimmed card cover. Attach the water-patterned paper inside the card with paper glue. The right edge of the water-patterned paper will remain visible when the card is closed.

two · Apply the cut fishing pole sticker to the vellum, then apply the handle sticker over the wide pole end. Punch a circle reel out of the black paper with the ⅝" (2cm) hole punch, then use the 1/16" (.2mm) punch to make a small hole in the center of the reel. Punch another small hole under the pole handle. Thread the mini brad through both holes to attach the reel to the front of the card. Working inside the card, separate the brad ends and lay them flat against the underside of the card cover.

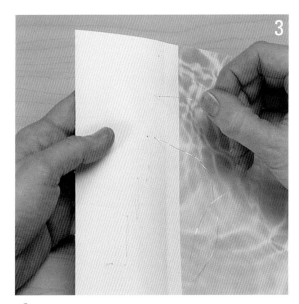

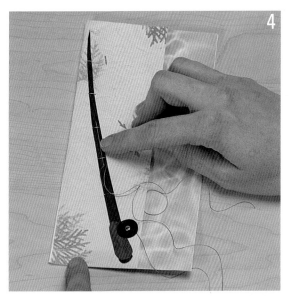

three · Use an awl to make five pairs of holes up the length of the rod, and a single hole at the tip of the rod. Starting inside the card thread the wire through the first hole above the handle. Stitch across the rod to connect the first pair of holes. Make a diagonal stitch inside the card to move the wire up to the next pair of holes. Continue working up the pole, connecting holes until you reach the single hole at the end. Make a small loop of wire through the last hole. Trim both wire ends and lay them flat inside the card.

four · Thread the blue thread onto the needle and tie the end around the brad, knotting it under the reel. Slide the needle under each wire loop to bring the fishing line all the way up the pole. Thread the needle through the top wire loop and then poke it down through the card cover. Remove the needle and allow the line to hang loosely inside the card. Apply the fish sticker to the water paper over the thread end. Position the fish so that it's partly visible when the card is closed.

*reel*

*rod*

*Pole and handle patterns, cut from wood grained sticker paper. Patterns are full size.*

# stamped leaf card

## MATERIALS

5½" x 8½" (14cm x 22cm) cream colored cardstock, folded to a 5½" x 4¼" (14cm x 11cm) card

green handmade tissue paper

4⅞" x 2" (12cm x 5cm) white handmade tissue paper

leaf stamp and stamp pad

plastic individual letter stickers

glue stick

basic tools (see page 8)

## MESSAGES

*Friend, Thank You, Fall, Thanksgiving, Love, Forever*

This card brings the outdoors inside without the hassle of pressing and preserving natural leaves. Made with realistic leaf stamps that are printed on natural fiber tissue papers, its elegant beauty is sure to impress.

ANOTHER SIMPLY BEAUTIFUL IDEA

Don't stop with just one stamp! Explore different leaf varieties and tissue paper colors. If your leaf stamp is smaller, make multiple prints on different colored papers. This project is so quick and easy that when you have the supplies out, consider assembling a whole packet of cards to give as a gift.

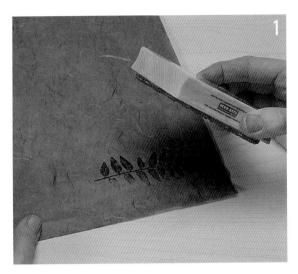

one · Because tissue paper is more porous than regular paper, work on a protected surface. Test print the stamp on scrap tissue paper first to get a feel for how much ink and pressure is required. When you're comfortable with the technique, stamp a leaf on the green handmade tissue paper.

two · Carefully tear around the outside of the stamped leaf to separate it from the rest of the sheet.

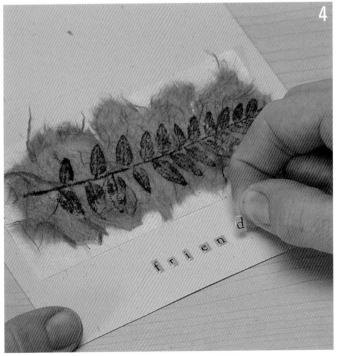

three · Orient the cream card horizontally and glue the white rectangle background slightly above the center of the card, then glue the stamped tissue paper leaf to the center of the background.

four · Spell your message with sticker letters below the white tissue paper background.

# spiderweb card

## MATERIALS

8" x 5½" (20cm x 14cm) striped scrapbook paper, folded to a 4" x 5½"
(10cm x 14cm) card

4" x 5½" (10cm x 14cm) white cardstock

3" x 4" (8cm x 10cm) green vellum

black thread

spider sticker

sewing needle

2" (5cm) circle template

shape cutter

awl

double-stick tape

paper glue

basic tools (see page 8)

## MESSAGES

*Happy Halloween, Eeek!,
Have a Creepy Crawly Good Time!*

S titching this spooky spider web couldn't be easier. Simply follow the steps to sew across the cut circle in the card cover. The eye-catching results will astound your friends.

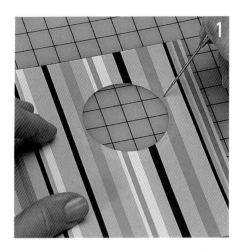

**one** · Use a shape cutter and shape template to cut a 2" (5cm) circle in the center front of your scrapbook paper card. Use an awl to make pairs of holes across the circle from each other. Position the holes ⅛" (3mm) from the edge of the circle, and space them ½" (1cm) apart from each other.

**two** · Thread the needle and knot the end of the thread. Starting inside the card, push the needle through a hole to the front of the card. Make a long stitch across the circle to the hole on the opposite side. On the inside of the card, make a small stitch to the neighboring hole and push the needle out to the front of the card. Continue working in this fashion until stitches have been made between each pair of punched holes. Knot the thread end inside the card and trim any excess.

**three** · Cut a new length of thread and tie one end in a knot around the center of the web threads. Thread the other end through the sewing needle. Loosely weave the needle in and out of the web threads to make a total of four concentric circles.

**four** · Let the end of the thread trail out the bottom of the web, then remove the needle. If necessary, trim the thread. Secure the end of the thread under a spider sticker.

**five** · Working inside the card, use double stick tape to adhere the green vellum background to the inside front cover. On the opposite side, glue the white cardstock piece over the scrapbook paper to strengthen the card.

# spinning spider card

## MATERIALS

5½" x 11" (14cm x 28cm) white cardstock, folded to a 5½" x 5½" (14cm x 14cm) card

spider pattern cut from orange patterned scrapbook paper

4¼" x 4¼" (11cm x 11cm) black patterned scrapbook paper

4¾" x 4¾" (12cm x 12cm) square of green paper

white copy paper

mini brad

fine-tip black marker

⅝" (2cm) circle paper punch

standard hole punch

paper glue

basic tools (see page 8)

## MESSAGES

*Boo!, Eeek!, Happy Halloween, Have a Creepy Good Time, You've Got Me Spinning*

Spin the eye-popping character on top of the card to watch it change expressions— eight times in a single rotation! This playful spook is fun for young and old alike. Use both the head and matching eyeball pattern to ensure your spinning success.

**one** · Use the pattern on page 110 as your guide to mark the exact placement of the center hole, two large eyeholes and six small eyeholes on the cut spider pattern. Invert the ⅝" (2cm) hole punch to verify that the punch is lined up with the marked eye placement, then punch the two large eyes. Punch the six remaining eyeholes with a standard-sized hole punch.

**two** · Outline all eight eyes and the entire outside edge of the spider pattern with the black marker. Next use the marker or a copy machine to re-create the spider eyeball pattern on white copy paper. Be sure to mark the exact placement of the center hole.

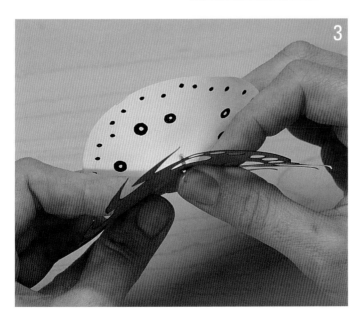

**three** · Trim the eye pattern so that it will fit under your rotating spider. Pierce a mini brad through the marked center hole on the spider's back, and then push it through the marked center hole in the eye pattern. Separate the brad ends and push them flush against the underside of the eye pattern, so the eye pattern is attached under the spider and the eyes can be seen through the spider's eyes.

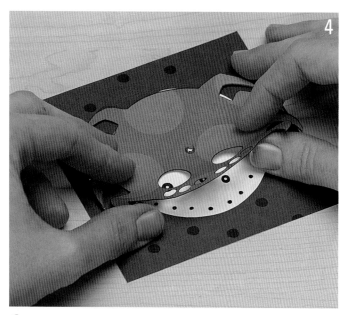

**four** • Apply glue to the underside of the eye pattern. Do not apply glue to the spider's legs, as it will prevent him from spinning. Press the finished spider to the center of the black paper square.

**five** • Glue the green paper square to the center of the card and then glue the black spider square over the center of the green square. To spin, turn the spider while holding the card.

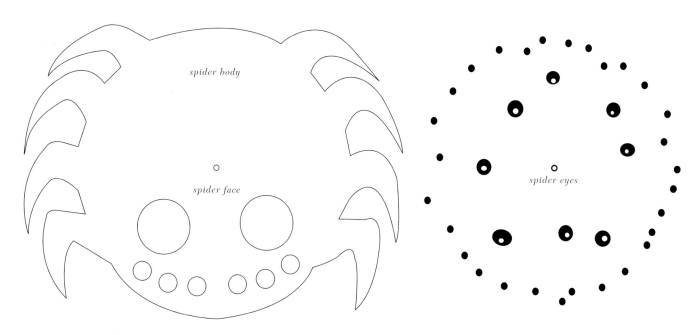

*spider body*

*spider face*

*spider eyes*

*Spider pattern cut from orange cardstock. Eye pattern is marked on white copy paper. Patterns are full size.*

# scaredy cat card

## MATERIALS

5½" x 11" (14cm x 28cm) white card-stock, folded to a 5½" x 5½" (14cm x 14cm) card

cat pattern cut from black scrapbook paper

4¼" x 4¼" (11cm x 11cm) black patterned scrapbook paper

4¾" x 4¾" (12cm x 12cm) square of green paper

green copy paper

mini brad

fine-tip white paint marker

⅝" (2cm) circle paper punch

paper glue

basic tools (see page 8)

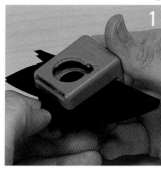

one • The black cat is cut from black paper. Outline the cat head with a white paint marker and draw the mouth, nose and whiskers Assemble the card as you did the Spinning Spider card on page 111. To punch out the eyes of the black cat, bring the sides of the head together and slide the hole punch over the folded paper. Make sure the hole punch lines up exactly with the previously marked eye placement. Carefully slide the paper free from the punch and flatten the head shape.

It might just be good luck to have this black cat cross your path before old Hallows Eve. More friendly than spooky, this cat's roving eyeballs make him a real head case.

*cat face*

*cat head*

*cat eyes*

*The cat eye pattern is labeled and cut from green copy paper. The cat head is cut from black scrapbook paper. Patterns are full size.*

# snowflake card

## MATERIALS

10¾" x 4" (27cm x 10cm) light blue paper

10¾" x 4" (27cm x 10cm) flecked copy paper

3" x 3¼" (8cm x 8cm) blue rice paper (torn edges for decorative effect)

3⅛" x 3⅞" (8cm x 10cm) silver cardstock

tiny white plastic marbles

letter stamps and white stamp pad

standard hole punch

glue stick

double-stick tape

double-sided adhesive sheet

basic tools (see page 8)

### MESSAGES

*Noel, Snow, Peace*

ANOTHER SIMPLY BEAUTIFUL IDEA

Let it snow! This year send wishes for a white Christmas. This snowflake is simply cut and punched from an adhesive sheet and is frosted with a sprinkling of tiny, lightweight plastic marbles. This is a clever way to capture the effect of an individual snowflake without the freezing temperatures.

No two snowflakes are alike! You can quickly and easily create a different snowflake card by changing the snowflake design. Individual letter stamps allow you to change the message at the bottom of the card to make each card unique.

one · Fold the blue paper in half vertically to make a 5⅜" x 4" (14cm x 10cm) card, then tear the top and bottom edges carefully. Slip a similarly folded sheet of white flecked copy paper inside the blue card. Use letter stamps and white ink to stamp a message just above the bottom edge of the blue card cover.

two · Cut the snowflake pattern from a sheet of double-sided adhesive. Punch holes in the pattern with a standard hand punch.

three · Peel the paper backing off one side of the snowflake and position it, adhesive side down, in the center of the rice paper. Remove the remaining paper backing and transfer the mounted snowflake to a shallow dish. Sprinkle tiny marbles onto the exposed adhesive. When done, tap the card over a dish to collect any stray marbles.

four · Use double-stick tape to attach the rice paper onto silver cardstock. Then glue the silver cardstock on the front of the card, just above the stamped message.

*Snowflake pattern cut from double sided adhesive. Pattern is full size.*

*tip* > To reach the holes at the center of the snowflake, try sliding the hole punch between the cut snowflake spikes.

# rhinestone tree

## MATERIALS

8" x 5½" (20cm x 14cm) white vellum, folded to a 4" x 5½" (10cm x 14cm) card

8" x 5½" (20cm x 14cm) white cardstock, folded to 4" x 5½" (10cm x 14cm) card

½" (1cm) length of ⅝" (2cm) red metallic ribbon

¾" (2cm) length of ¼" (1cm) silver ribbon

assorted red and white plastic rhinestones

star shaped stud

fine-point black marker

scrapbook glue

embellishment glue

tree pattern

basic tools (see page 8)

### MESSAGES

*Merry Christmas, Happy Holidays, Season's Greetings*

ANOTHER SIMPLY BEAUTIFUL IDEA

Know someone who needs a little holiday spirit? Send them a miniature tree that doesn't need to be plugged in to twinkle. This card is simply elegant, and quick and easy enough to make for everyone on your holiday card list. Layer vellum over a folded white cardstock card, and then add sparkle with rhinestones.

Making this welcoming wreath is a simple alternative to the tree. Draw a wreath pattern onto the white card, and then glue green and white rhinestones on the vellum. Add a red bow to the vellum card cover.

one · Draw the tree pattern with black marker on the front of the white cardstock card. Use scrapbook glue to attach the piece of red ribbon to the base of the tree and the silver ribbon over the top edge of the red ribbon.

two · Slide the finished tree card into the vellum card.

three · Push the star shaped stud into the vellum card, positioning it over the top of the tree. Working inside the vellum card, push down the pointed stud ends so they lie flat against the vellum. Use embellishment glue to apply rhinestones to the front of the vellum card, arranging them as ornaments between the branches. Let the glue dry completely before mailing.

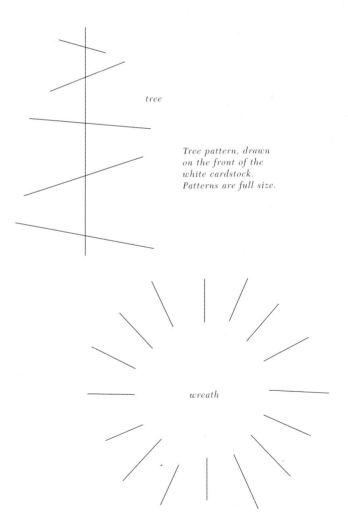

*tree*

Tree pattern, drawn
on the front of the
white cardstock.
Patterns are full size.

*wreath*

# cold hands, warm hearts

## MATERIALS

two mitten patterns cut from
light green cardstock

large heart and cuffs cut from
black paper

small heart cut from floral patterned
scrapbook paper

lowercase alphabet stamps and black
stamp pad

7" (18cm) embroidery floss

two white feathers

needle

scallop-edged scissors

¹⁄₁₆" (.2mm) hole punch

paper glue

scrapbook glue

basic tools (see page 8)

Reminiscent of fur-lined Inuit mittens, this holiday card can be hung from a tree branch as an ornament or even used as a gift tag. No sewing is required, as the clever stitching is actually made with lowercase letter stamps.

A simple change in the color of the cardstock, and some carefully chosen scrapbook paper, can make a card appropriate for everyone on your holiday card-giving list.

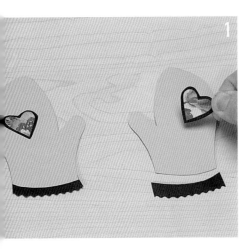

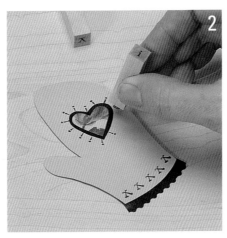

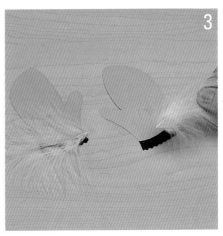

one · Flip one of the mittens over so both thumbs face inward. Use scallop-edged scissors to cut the bottom edge of the black cuff. Use paper glue to attach the following cut pattern pieces to the mitten: a black cuff under the bottom edge of each mitten, a floral heart to the center of each black heart, and the combined hearts to the middle of each mitten.

two · Repeatedly stamp a lowercase *i* around the black heart edge to simulate straight appliqué stitches. Make a row of *x* stamps above the mitten cuffs to simulate a line of decorative cross-stitching.

three · Flip the mittens over and apply a line of scrapbook glue along the top edge of the black cuffs. Prepare the feathers by cutting off the quill ends and then press a feather into each line of glue so that soft feathers extend below the cuff edge.

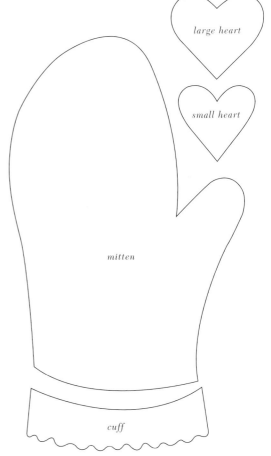

*large heart*

*small heart*

*mitten*

*cuff*

four · Turn the mittens right side up and punch a hole in the outside edge of each mitten cuff. Thread the needle with the entire thickness of embroidery floss. Bring the needle up through the punched hole in the left mitten. Draw the floss through the hole, stopping to knot the floss end back around itself beside the hole. Allow the length of floss to span between the two mittens. Thread the needle through the hole in the right hand mitten. Remove the needle and knot the other end of the floss.

*Mitten cut from green cardstock. Large heart cut from black paper, small heart cut from scrapbook paper and cuff cut from black paper. Patterns are full size.*

# holiday sparkle

## MATERIALS

5½" x 11" (14cm x 28cm) white card-stock, folded to a 5½" x 5½" (14cm x 14cm) card

5½" x 5½" (14cm x 14cm) metallic green origami paper

ornament base pattern cut from red foil cardstock

ornament decoration patterns cut from red and two varieties of gold holographic sticker sheets

2½" (6cm) length of 20-gauge wire

gold mini brad fastener

3⅝" (9cm) circle template

shape cutter

1/16" (.2mm) hole punch

roundnose pliers

paper glue

basic tools (see page 8)

## MESSAGES

*Seasons Greetings, Merry Christmas, Happy Holidays*

This sparkling ornament catches the light as it spins in the cut opening. Holographic sticker sheets add dimension to the otherwise flat paper ornament. They are easy to use. Just cut, peel and stick!

**This sparkling ornament is also designed to slip off the front of the card and to hang on the Christmas tree.**

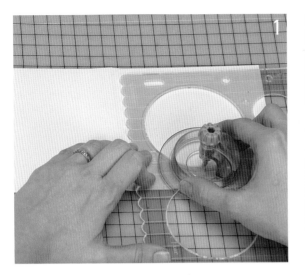

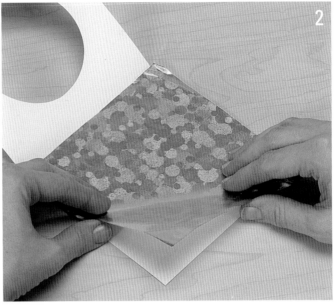

one • Use the shape cutter and template to cut the 3⅝" (9cm) circle opening out of the front of the card.

two • Glue the metallic green origami paper inside the card, so the foil shows through the circle you just cut in the card.

*tip* > If you don't have a shape cutter, use a compass or trace around the bottom of a glass or small bowl to mark the circle opening in the card. Then use a craft knife to cut the circle out.

three • Cut out the base ornament pattern on page 121 from red foil cardstock. The remaining pattern pieces are cut from holographic sticker sheets. Begin assembling the ornament by attaching the zigzagged sticker to the right edge of the base.

four · Apply the remaining stickers, working from largest to smallest, until you have assembled the holographic ornament.

five · Punch a hole in the front of the card, ¼" (1cm) above the center of the cut circle edge. Then punch a hole at the top of the ornament.

six · Thread the wire through the ornament. Use roundnose pliers to bend the short wire end up in front of the ornament and shape it into a small spiral. Bend the longer end up behind the ornament and shape it into a larger spiral.

seven · Thread a brad through the punched hole in the card and separate the ends inside the card.

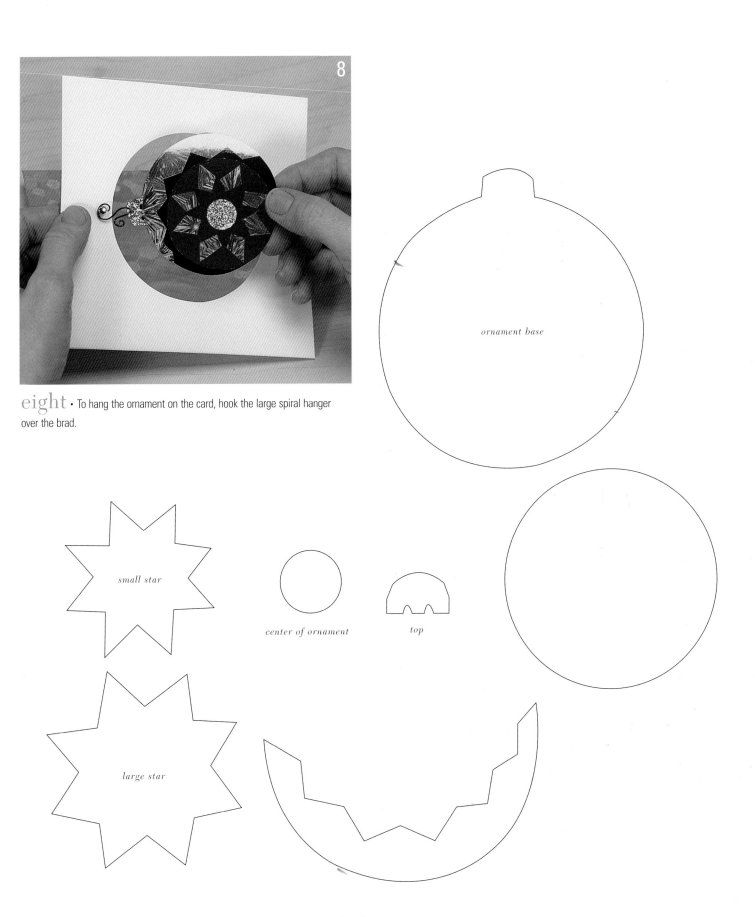

eight · To hang the ornament on the card, hook the large spiral hanger over the brad.

*ornament base*

*small star*

*center of ornament*

*top*

*large star*

Cut the base ornament from red foil cardstock. The remaining ornament pieces are cut from red and gold foil scrapbook stickers. Patterns are full size.

# winter wonderland

## MATERIALS

8" x 5½" (20cm x 14cm) white cardstock, folded to a 4" x 5½" (10cmx14cm) card

white cardstock scraps for snowdrifts pattern

8" x 5½" (20cm x 14cm) green cardstock, folded to a 4" x 5½" (10cm x 14cm) card

green cardstock scraps for trees

sky pattern cut from dark blue origami paper (flecked with gold and silver)

animal stickers

letter stamps and stamp pad

star hand punch

paper glue

basic tools (see page 8)

## MESSAGES

*Peace, Happy Holidays, Winter Wonderland*

This card will appeal to the child in everyone. When opened, it transports you to a starlit forest where small animals frolic in the snowy winter landscape. Straight cuts, triangular trees and stickers keep this three-dimensional card simple to make.

one · Use the letter stamps to add a message to the inside lower half of the white card.

two · Refold the white card and place the pattern from page 125 against the outside, lining it up along the folded edge. Trace and cut eight slits through both layers of the card.

three · Open the card and push the four strips you just made into the card. This will reverse their center folds, so that they pop out inside the card.

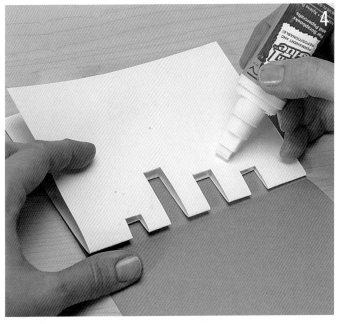

four · Glue the white card inside the green card. Be careful not to apply glue to the four pop-out strips, as this will ruin the three-dimensional effect.

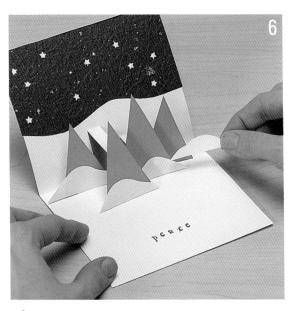

five · Use a hand punch to create stars in the origami sky. Apply glue to the back of the sky and position it on the inside of the card. Line up the white and blue top and side edges. The white cardstock will show through where the stars were punched.

six · Glue trees on the front side of each of the pop outs. Make sure you apply glue to the white paper and not the trees. Then glue a white snowdrift to the base of each tree.

seven · Apply animal stickers to the bottom of each snowdrift. Apply a small animal sticker to the stamped message on the card.

eight · Make use of your paper scraps to decorate the front of the card. Start with a dark blue sky background and white snowdrift. Then apply a deer sticker onto the newly created background. Punch stars from white scrap paper and glue them onto the green and blue background.

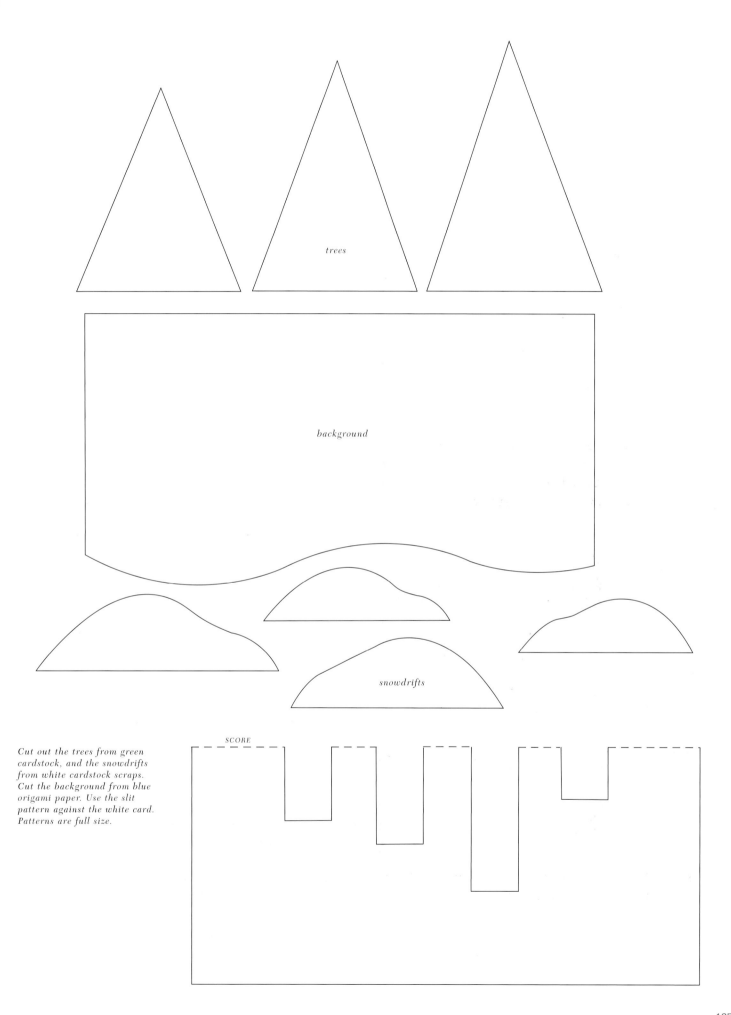

trees

background

snowdrifts

SCORE

Cut out the trees from green cardstock, and the snowdrifts from white cardstock scraps. Cut the background from blue origami paper. Use the slit pattern against the white card. Patterns are full size.

125

# resources

**ACCENT FACTORY**
- *Metal embellishments (pgs. 34, 36 and 38)*

**AMERICAN ART CLAY CO.**
(800) 374-1600
www.amaco.com
- *Wire mesh and fine-mesh metalscreens (pgs. 18 and 24)*

**CREATIVE IMAGINATIONS, INC**
(800) 942-6487
www.cigift.com
- *Scrapbook alphabet and other stickers (pgs. 34 and 36)*

**DUNCAN**
(800) 438-6226
www.duncancrafts.com
- *Aleene's 2 and 1 Paper Glue, Aleene's Memory Glue, Aleene's Platinum Bond Glass and Bead Glue, Tulip Dimensional Paint, sticker sheets and other adhesives and crafting products*

**FISKARS**
(847) 590-0500
www.fiskars.com
- *ShapeCutter and circle cutter, decorative scissors, hand punches, craft knife and embossing tool*

**HALCRAFT**
(212) 376-1580
www.halcraft.com
- *Beads and marbles*

**HERO ARTS**
www.heroarts.com
- *Alphabet stamps (pgs. 70, 72, 116 and 122)*

**HIRSCHBERG SHUTZ & CO., INC.**
(908) 810-1111
- *Decorative stickers (pg. 74)*

**K & COMPANY**
(816) 389-4150
www.kandcompany.com
- *Scrapbook letter stickers and papers (pgs. 50, 52 and 104)*

**MAKING MEMORIES**
(801) 294-0430
www.makingmemories.com
- *Scrapbook and metal embellishments, metal glue (pgs. 62 and 76)*

**MARVY UCHIDA**
(800) 541-5877
www.uchida.com
- *Cirlce, star and heart paper punches*

**ME & MY BIG IDEAS**
www.meandmybigideas.com
- *Threads and woven labels (pg. 76)*

**MRS. GROSSMAN'S PAPER COMPANY**
(800) 429-4549
www.mrsgrossmans.com
- *Decorative stickers (pgs. 54 and 122)*

**PEBBLES, INC.**
(801) 235-1520
www.pebblesinc.com
- *Color labels and other embellishments (pg. 66)*

**PLAID ENTERPRISES, INC.**
(800) 842-4197
www.plaidonline.com
- *Decorative and alphabet stamps, Modge Podge and Anna Griffin scrapbook papers and stamps (pgs. 40, 58, 72, 74, 78, 81, 86, 104 and 112)*

**PSX**
(866) 779-9877
www.psxdesign.com
- *Alphabet stamp (pg. 18)*

**SCRAPBOOK HERITAGE**
www.scrapbookheritage.com.au
- *Naturally gifted scrapboook stickers (pgs. 24, 50, 96, 99 and 102)*

**S.E.I**
(800) 333-3279
www.shopsei.com
- *Decorative scrapbook papers and stickers (pg. 22)*

**STICKOPOTAMUS**
- *Decorative scrapbook stickers (pgs. 45 and 106)*

**XYRON**
(800) 457-9566
www.xyron.com
- *Repositionable tape*

# index

**A**
Adhesives, 8
Awl, 9

**B**
Beads, 12
Blank card, making, 14
Bone folder, 9
Buttons, 12

**C**
Cardstock, 10
Computer-generated type, 13
Craft knife, 9

**D**
Decorative scissors, 9

**E**
Embellishment glue, 8
Embossing tool, 8
Envelopes, 11
Eyelet setter, 9
Eyelets, 12

**H**
Handmade paper, 10
Handwriting, 13
Holiday cards, 90-125
Holographic sticker sheets, 11

**I**
Introduction, 7

**M**
Marker, 8
Materials
    beads, 12
    buttons, 12
    embroidery floss, 12
    eyelets, 12
    mesh, 12
    mini brad fasteners, 12
    paper. see Paper
    ribbon, 12
    silk flowers, 12
    type. see Type
    wire, 12
Mesh, 12
Mini brad fasteners, 12

**O**
Origami, 10

**P**
Paper
    cardstock, 10
    envelopes, 11
    finding, 10-11
    handmade, 10
    holographic sticker sheets, 11
    origami, 10
    patterned scrapbook, 10
    pre-folded cards, 11
    storing, 10-11
    suede, 10
    textured, 10
    tissue, 10
    vellum, 10
Paper glue, 8
Paper punches, 9
Paper trimmer, 8
Patterned scrapbook paper, 10
Patterns, 15
Pencil, 8
Personal cards, 16-55
Pre-folded cards, 11

**R**
Repositionable glue tape, 8
Resources, 126
Ribbon, 12
Ribbon roses, finding, 69
Houndnose pliers, 9
Ruler, 8

**S**
Scissors, 8
Scrapbook glue, 8
Seasonal cards, 90-125
Self-healing cutting board, 9
Shape cutter and shape template, 9
Signing your cards, 14
Silk flowers, 12
Special event cards, 60-93
Stamps, 13
Stickers, 13
Suede paper, 10
Suppliers, 126

**T**
Techniques
    blank card, making, 14
    patterns, cutting, 15
    stamping, 15
Textured paper, 10
Tissue paper, 10
Tools
    adhesives, 8
    awl, 9
    bone folder, 9
    craft knife, 9
    decorative scissors, 9
    embellishment glue, 8
    embossing tool, 8
    eyelet setter, 9
    marker, 8
    paper glue, 8
    paper punches, 9
    paper trimmer, 8
    pencil, 8
    repositionable glue tape, 8
    roundnose pliers, 9
    ruler, 8
    scissors, 8
    scrapbook glue, 8
    self-healing cutting board, 9
    shape cutter and shape template, 9
Type
    computer-generated type, 13
    handwriting, 13
    stamps, 13
    stickers, 13

**V**
Vellum, 10

**W**
Wire, 12

# TRY YOUR HAND AT THESE OTHER FUN CRAFTS WITH GUIDANCE FROM NORTH LIGHT BOOKS!

THESE BOOKS AND OTHER FINE NORTH LIGHT TITLES are available from your local art & craft retailer, bookstore, online supplier or by calling 1-800-448-0915.

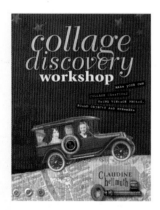

### COLLAGE DISCOVERY WORKSHOP

Open a new world of creativity with Collage Discovery Workshop. You'll learn how to create distinct collages through 12 step-by-step projects, creative exercises and journaling prompts. To enhance your pieces, you'll find 15 innovative and unique techniques for antiquing objects, transferring images and creating amazing backgrounds. Among the projects included are collaged tin refrigerator magnets, beeswax collages and shadowboxes. ISBN 1-58180-343-5, paperback, 128 pages, #32313

### GREETING CARDS FOR EVERY OCCASION

Renowed crafter MaryJo McGraw shares her most creative card ideas. With complete, step-by-step instructions and 23 detailed projects, it's easy to make your sentiments more personal and meaningful. You'll find a wealth of inspiring card ideas for nearly every holiday and occasion, including Christmas, Valentine's Day, Mother's and Father's Day, birthday, get well soon, new job and much more! ISBN 1-58180-410-5, paperback, 128 pages, #32580-K

### BRIGHT IDEAS IN PAPERCRAFTS

Bring a personal touch to every celebration, holiday and special occasion. Bright Ideas in Papercrafts gives guidelines and advice for creating 23 elegant projects using all of your favorite tools, from decorative edging scissors to paper crimpers, archival papers and more. It's easy, fun and fast! Start creating handcrafted keepsakes that will be treasured for years to come. ISBN 1-58180-352-4, paperback, 128 pages, #32325-K

### CREATIVE CORRESPONDENCE

You can create spectacular decorative mail! You'll find 15 step-by-step projects including letters and envelopes with photo inserts, stapled booklets, and acetate address windows, plus clever self-mailers. With the basic techniques, embellishments and decorative techniques demonstrated inside, you'll achieve great-looking results from start to finish. ISBN 1-58180-317-6, paperback, 96 pages, #32277-K